*Explorations in World Ethnology*

ROBERT B. EDGERTON and L. L. LANGNESS
University of California, Los Angeles

General Editors

# The Himalayan Woman

## A STUDY OF LIMBU WOMEN
## IN MARRIAGE AND DIVORCE

*Rex L. Jones and Shirley Kurz Jones*

 MAYFIELD PUBLISHING COMPANY

*To Mahali, friend and assistant,*
*and to a learned*
*Limbu historian,*
*Nar Bir Tumbahangphe*

Library of Congress Catalog Card Number: 76-28117
International Standard Book Number: 0-87484-379-0

Manufactured in the United States of America
Mayfield Publishing Company
285 Hamilton Avenue, Palo Alto, California 94301

This book was set in Palatino and Crayonette by Publications
Services and was printed and bound by Publishers Press.
Sponsoring editor was Alden C. Paine, Carole Norton supervised editing, and Michelle Hogan supervised production. The
book and cover were designed by Nancy Sears.

# Contents

# Preface

Today in America and Europe, women's rights are very much on people's minds. Because women are so vocal—even militant—about these topics, men cannot ignore them, nor can they avoid frequent public and private discussions about the "woman's role" in society. To us, the women's movement is not a passing fad or simply one more temporary problem of a fast-changing technological society. We believe it might well be one of the most far-reaching revolutionary changes in human history, and for that reason it behooves us to learn as much as we can about women's lives everywhere.

The women's movement in Europe and America is primarily directed toward inequalities in salaries, jobs, education, and decision making; but much of the outcry focuses on the customary view of women in family life, the home, and the community. Many women who do not see themselves only as child-bearers, baby-sitters, and homemakers are challenging two traditions: women's conventional functions in Western society and men's and women's roles in the process of human evolution. Such questioning is making us rethink outmoded conceptions of how we became what we are now, and the parts men and women have played throughout history. These concerns have been uppermost in our thoughts during the writing of this book.

Of course, the women's movement is correct to question the division of human behavior into stereotyped ideas of what is "male" and what is "female." Differences in men's and women's behavior certainly do exist, but they vary according to society and culture. This point of view is basic to our discussions throughout *The Himalayan Woman.*

The theme of our book is women's roles, especially in marriage and divorce, in Limbuan, a community in the Nepal Himalaya. In portraying women more extensively than men we do not mean to suggest that we feel women are more important in Limbu society. Our reason is that women's roles are often taken for granted by anthropologists writing on south Asia, most of whom are men writing about male subjects. We also hope to dispel stereotyped thinking about the woman's "place" in that part of the world.

Our topic was chosen for three reasons. First, since much of our initial interest as anthropologists was in the field of marriage and the family, we acquired a great deal of information about that aspect of Limbu society. Second, because marriage and the family are institutions that may reach back as far as the beginning of human culture itself, they are good starting points in discussing men and women in any society. Third, Limbu marriage and the family are intrinsically fascinating because of the importance women seem to have in maintaining a successful marriage and a fruitful family life. The stability of Limbu marriage and the structure of the family are directly related to Limbu women's other activities at home and in the community.

We consider that marriage is a process rather than an act, involving not only the motivations and goals of husband and wife but those of the ambient society as a whole. We view with skepticism the findings of studies that purport to describe marriage stability and instability within a society solely on the basis of divorce rates. Such data afford a very static, unidimensional picture of marriage and family life. Thus, although we have not ignored divorce statistics altogether, our study is based heavily on personal contacts with the Limbu people and on participant observation.

Our research for *The Himalayan Woman* was first undertaken from 1967 to 1969. In that period we learned how the Limbu lived on a day-to-day basis and gathered most of the material in the case histories of marriage and divorce presented in chapter 5. These data were supplemented by the collection of ten genealogies which revealed a wide spectrum of marriages in past generations. We then formulated hypotheses and questions concerning Limbu marriage and divorce and women's roles, which were tested in the fall of 1975 in systematic interviews of eighty-six married women in three adjacent Limbu villages.

We would like to thank the Limbu people for their cooperation and hospitality during our stay with them. We also appreciate the help we received from the Nepal government and various Peace Corps volunteers during our trip, in particular the mail service they provided and the medical aid at various points in our fieldwork.

The initial research was financed by ourselves. For subsequent research and completion of this book, Rex Jones would like to thank the State University of New York Research Foundation for a Summer Fellowship and Research Grant; and The American Council of Learned Societies and The Social Science Research Council for a grant which also helped finance a follow-up trip to gather information on the economic independence of Limbu women. Material from that trip has been incorporated throughout the text.

For assistance in our education, research, and writing, we are indebted to teachers, colleagues, students, friends, and family. To list them all would be impossible. Rex would like to thank especially Gene Hodges, a life-long friend, who first interested him in the study of anthropology. John Hitchcock, William Bright, Pedro Carrasco, and Robert Edgerton have been our teachers as graduate students, and we are particularly grateful to them. We thank Louis Faron, Richard Gardner, Nina Jody, Stavroula Christodoulou, Peter Brown, William Arens, and Theodore Kennedy for reading the manuscript and offering helpful comments. For clerical help and time-consuming labor in the preparation and editing of the manuscript, we would like to thank Edith Matlock, Mari Walker, Nancy Johnson, and Linda Brandt. We alone are responsible for the final contents of the book.

Finally, we would like to express our gratitude and appreciation to our parents, Harry and Yeta Kurz, Kenneth Jones and Mary Haile, for their encouragement and financial help in our education and research.

# Editors' Preface

It is widely recognized in anthropology circles that anthropological studies of traditional societies have been oriented more to the activities and beliefs of men than women. This research imbalance has persisted despite the fact that many of the most distinguished anthropologists have been women. In recent years anthropologists have attempted to correct the situation by looking more closely at the role of women. This book by Rex and Shirley Jones is a contribution toward that end. It examines the social role of women in Limbuan, a community in the Himalayan Mountains of Nepal. Although the Joneses focused their research primarily on women, they recognize that the lives of men and women in all societies are inseparably linked; thus in this book they also tell us a great deal about how men and women live together in Limbu society.

Perhaps because Nepal was not open to Western scholars before the 1950's, it remains in the minds of most Westerners an exotic and romantic place. The Joneses tell us of their quite personal feelings about doing research there, detailing the culture shock they experienced when they first arrived in a society so different from their own. But the bulk of their book is about the ways in which Limbu women relate to men in courtship, marriage, economic roles, and divorce. Unlike high-caste Hindu women in southern Asia, Limbu women are relatively free to divorce, remarry, possess a personal income, and sometimes even own property. The Joneses not only describe in detail the activities of these women; they also attempt to explain why they are by no means subservient to men. In their own words, "The woman in south Asia is not typically a passive, shy, and secluded creature, but more often an active participant in the economy and social life of the village. In many regions, the woman has a culturally recognized right to make significant and far-reaching decisions about her own life, decisions which may have repercussions in many other areas of the society. We are not saying that Limbu women, or any women in south Asia, have achieved an ideal state of equality with men and a total independence in public activities. But their independence has frequently been overlooked and misunderstood. We hope that this book will have an impact on future research in the area, and on the already changing view of the role of women in marriage and the family."

Rex L. Jones received his Ph.D. in anthropology from the University of California, Los Angeles, in 1973. Since 1972 he has taught in the Department of Anthropology at the State University of New York at Stony Brook. In addition to his research in Nepal, which has led to numerous publications, he has done research with various Southern California Indians, and since 1969 he has studied poker clubs in Southern California.

Shirley Kurz Jones has done post-graduate studies at UCLA, The University of Wisconsin, and the State University of New York at Stony Brook. She returned to Nepal in the summer of 1976 to collect a series of life histories of Limbu women. This research will form the basis of her doctoral dissertation.

Robert B. Edgerton
L. L. Langness

# THE HIMALAYAN WOMAN

*Hajur!*

> *When there is a fire in the forest*
> *all men can see it,*
> *When there is a fire inside you,*
> *only you and God can see it!*

> (*a Limbu dance song*)

# *Meeting the People*

# *1*

As young anthropology graduate students in the early 1960s, we were captivated by the idea of doing field work in an exotic society thousands of miles away from Los Angeles. With its mountains and ten to twelve million people, some of whom thought America was "near London" which was "near Kashmir," Nepal seemed an ideal place for us to live out our fantasies.

When we began our field work in Nepal in 1967, the country and its people were still inadequately described in the literature of the West. Most of what was known about Nepalese lifestyles and beliefs was based on reports and descriptions by authors who had never been to Nepal, or who had visited only briefly. This was our chief reason for choosing to study the Limbu. Shortly after our arrival, we learned that a French ethnographer, Philippe Sagant, was also working with the Limbu, and that Lionel Caplan had just completed a research project among the Limbu of Ilam district. Today, even after field work by anthropologists from France, Great Britain, Germany, the United States, Japan, Australia, Italy, India, and Nepal itself, the Nepalese are still living relatively isolated lives and are not well understood by Westerners.

Nepal opened its doors to Westerners and scholars in 1951, yet throughout the 1950s and early 1960s only a handful of ethnographers had ventured into the hill areas for systematic research. Professor Christoph von Fürer-Haimendorf of the University of London, who con-

1

ducted extensive field work among tribal groups in India, was one of the pioneers. In the 1950s he conducted research on high-caste Hindu groups and the Newar in the Kathmandu valley of Nepal and then investigated the Sherpa, a Tibetan-speaking people near Mount Everest who achieved fame in mountaineering expeditions. Fürer-Haimendorf wrote one of the first full-scale ethnographies of a Nepali people in 1964.

At the School of Oriental & African Studies in London, under Professor Fürer-Haimendorf's direction, a number of ethnographers began research on eastern and central Nepal. Colin Rosser (1966) wrote an excellent article on the Newar caste system, and Lionel Caplan completed a Ph.D. dissertation on the Limbu, which was later revised and published (Caplan 1970). Charles Macdougal had conducted a year's research among the Rai in 1964–65 but had not yet published his work.

French ethnographers of the Centre d'Etudes Nepalaises of the Centre National de la Recherches Scientifique in Paris were exploring the ethnographic hinterlands, but much of the material at that time was still unpublished. Bernard Pignède's study (1966) of the Gurung appeared at that time, and other scholars, including A. W. Macdonald, Corneille Jest, Marc Gaborieau, and Mireille Helffer, were researching and publishing in scholarly French journals. These scholars continue to produce ethnographic investigations on the Nepal people.

Japanese ethnographers and geographers had made a brief investigation of parts of western Nepal, but did not follow this up with systematic ethnographies. In addition, Professor John Hitchcock of the United States, in a book published in 1966, had described a Tibeto-Burman-speaking group in western Nepal, the Magar, and he and his wife Pat had made four films of the area.

Classical scholars, Tibetologists, linguists, historians, and political scientists had begun to describe the Nepal Valley and its literary tradition to Westerners, but the ethnography of the hill people, who were largely illiterate, seemed very sketchy to us. Nepal and its cultural and linguistic diversity presented one of the few remaining challenges to anthropologists who wanted the romance of investigating a relatively unknown culture.

Our interest in Nepal began in 1965 under the tutelage of Professor John Hitchcock, who was then teaching in the Anthropology Department at UCLA. After serving as Professor Hitchcock's research assistant in 1964, Rex switched his interest from Africa to Asia almost immediately. Until then, he had probably not heard the name "Nepal" more than half a dozen times and would have had difficulty locating the country on the map. Like so many Americans, he vaguely associated the word with Mount Everest, the tallest mountain in the world, and with the famous Gurkha soldiers of World Wars I and II. But Professor Hitchcock began to give him reading lists on the area, and in June 1965 Rex completed a master's essay entitled, "Cultural Diversity in the Himalayas." By the time Rex met Shirley that summer, he had received a 1960s "Sputnik Grant" (NDEA Title II Language Fellowship) to study the Nepali language and South Asian history at the University of Pennsylvania.

During the following two years, the two of us began to formulate a research plan that would take us to Nepal. The project that ultimately emerged from this planning was conceived as a cooperative effort. Rex concentrated on genealogical data, patterns of descent, and kinship terminology. Shirley focused on case studies, supplemented by genealogical charts or "family trees." Because so little had been published, our project was extremely flexible.

After we had set up housekeeping, we discovered that most Nepali women in the hills had never seen a Western woman. Throughout our field work, Shirley was an object of intense curiosity. She was the first woman anthropologist to visit Limbuan, and even the men, who were more worldly wise than the women because they had served with the army in different countries, were puzzled as to Shirley's intentions. At first Shirley wore trousers and boots, and this manner of dressing provoked amazed cries of "What is it, a man or a woman?" Shirley also wore glasses, and in the hills of Nepal where women seldom could afford such amenities, these glasses became a status symbol. Later, as people pestered us to take photographs, the women asked Shirley to let them wear the glasses for the photograph.

Shirley's excellent rapport with Limbu women not only resulted in the valuable "female-oriented" data on marriage stability incorporated in this book, but also influenced the direction of our investigations. We decided to examine the lives of women more than those of men because the information we were getting made us realize to what extent women had been overlooked in anthropological studies concerned with Nepal and India. The probable reason for this oversight, we concluded, is that most of those works were written by male anthropologists who more often interviewed male subjects.

Because marriage and kinship was from the outset a great interest of ours, we gathered more information on that aspect of Limbu society than any other. The institution of marriage may have started at the beginning of culture itself, and it is therefore an excellent jumping-off place for discussing the roles of men and women in any society. Finally, in Limbuan the institution of marriage is intrinsically interesting because of the significant part the women of that society play in marital stability and change.

## Method of Analysis

For the purpose of this study, marriage is defined as the legalized union of a man and woman that may produce legitimate offspring. We assess marriage stability not in simple terms of cohabitation and divorce, but rather in terms of *the degree to which a legally married couple maintains compatible conjugal relations free from long-term separations.*

A number of studies in anthropology have dealt with the subject of marriage stability. Early hypotheses were built on the use of the "divorce rate" as an indicator of marriage stability (Gluckman 1950; Fallers 1957; Leach 1957; and Lewis 1962). Attempts were made to link high divorce rates to patterns of descent (Gluckman 1950), or to the varying degrees to which a woman is integrated into her husband's descent group (Leach 1957; Fallers 1957; and Lewis 1962).

Limbu divorce rates, we found, cannot be calculated in terms of a ratio of marriages to divorces in a single year, since such statistics are unavailable. One study which correlated the number of recorded divorces and marriages in a sample cluster of villages (Caplan 1970:84) estimates Limbu divorce rates at 19.8 percent. Jones (1973:207) estimates the divorce rate from genealogical data at 13.4 percent of recorded marriages. A later study by Rex Jones in 1975, based on interviews of married women in three adjacent villages, revealed that 21 percent had been divorced at least once. On the basis of these data we can therefore estimate that Limbu divorce rates range from 13 to 21 percent. Compared to many societies, these percentages are extremely high; compared to American divorce rates in recent years, the figures are somewhat low.

Theories that treat the divorce rate alone as an indicator of marriage stability have been criticized sharply by Schneider (1953) and Cohen (1961). Schneider (1953:55) argues that this single indicator theory leads to confusion between "jural relations" and "conjugal relations," or situations in which a marriage is not broken legally even though the couple separate, as among the Nuer (Evans-Pritchard 1951). Clearly a separation between spouses can be an unstable marriage in the most elementary sense and yet never be revealed in divorce statistics.

There are a number of other problems involved in an analysis of marriage stability using the divorce rate as an indicator. Divorce rates conceal cultural meanings in marriage stability and lead to mistakes on a theoretical level. As indicated by Lloyd (1968:71),

> A divorce rate, expressed as a ratio of divorces to marriages, is but an imperfect indication of marriage stability. A high rate may result from an indulgence in trial marriages (as among the Tallensi, for instance), after which each couple remains united until death. Equally, a high rate may result from the rapid circulation of a few sterile women; Lewis (1962:35), while giving a structural explanation of the Somali divorce rate, describes infertility as the principal cause of divorce and adds that barren women usually experience a series of short unions. Yet again, a high rate may arise when women return to their home compounds after menopause, as among the Gonja (Goody 1962). The matrilineal Ndembu have a very high rate of divorce; but it is their practice to divorce a chronically sick spouse in order to evade the obligations of a surviving partner (Turner 1957: 263).

We have attempted to incorporate these warnings into our analysis. The rate of Limbu divorce does not tell us the complete story of Limbu marriage stability since a Limbu marriage represents a form of "trial marriage" in the legal sense. The marriage may only be finalized at the death of the woman or up to fifteen years after the betrothal ceremony with the final marriage payment. At that time the Limbu woman assumes the clan name of her husband, and in effect loses her rights or claims to the property of her natal family. The Limbu recognize divorce before this final payment, both normatively, in that either a man or woman has the right to end a marriage after the betrothal ceremony, and realistically, in that a marriage ended after the initial brideprice payment must be followed by compensation and legal proceedings.

Between betrothal and the dissolution of a marriage, either through death or divorce, events may occur in the marriage and in the families of the husband and wife which will contribute to the stability of the marriage bond. To evaluate these forces, the observer must study the kinship system as a whole and the function that kinship behavior has in the total context of political and economic relations. The motivations, goals, and rewards of the individuals should be considered against the total background of cultural values. Idiosyncracies and individual pathologies that might contribute to marriage instability in a few instances will then stand out clearly.

Through a study of marriage case histories, a profile of the marriage process as it is "played out" by specific individuals emerges. The danger in this method lies in the choice of examples. The ethnographer may only be presented with cases from a particular village or region, which may represent a provincial, economic, or political bias. We fully realized in writing this book that our description of Limbu marriage, divorce, and the woman's role in this process might embody such a bias, inasmuch as our own field experience took place primarily in the Tehrathum area of eastern Nepal. In order to offset this possibility and to round out as much as possible our own experiences and research, we have carefully taken note of the published work of the French ethnographer Philippe Sagant, who lived to the north of us, and the Canadian anthropologist Lionel Caplan, who worked in an entirely different area to the southeast.

The case studies we have used illustrate a broad range of situations in which Limbu men and women marry and divorce. The use of the case-history method allows the investigator to depict both what is expected in marriage by the society as a whole and what actually takes place. The method therefore helps us to understand to what degree individuals conform to the jural and moral rules that govern marriage and divorce—to assess what anthropologists often call "the difference between ideal and actual behavior." (See Schneider 1953; Cohen 1961.) Obviously, a consideration of divorce rates alone could not give us this kind of understanding.


## Finances and Research Permission

Beginning research students in anthropology face two basic problems that are less troublesome to the well established anthropologist: financing, and obtaining permission to study in a foreign country. For two years prior to field work we wrote grant proposals, all of which were rejected. We finally decided to finance the research on our own and in a year had saved, borrowed and scraped together enough money for a two-year round-the-world trip. (This venture, including transportation to and from Nepal, was actually less expensive than two years in the United States would have been.)

Obtaining a research visa in Nepal proved to be extremely difficult. Like many countries, Nepal does not grant such a visa until the student's intentions, background, and plans for publishing the information collected are thoroughly examined. Moreover, because Nepal will not grant a visa until after the would-be researcher arrives in the country, one needs a good deal more than a passport and identification on arrival. The government demands clearance of the research proposal through its channels, scrutinizes the procedures and sources of funding, and asks for

*6*

confirmation from the American Consulate. For us, cutting through red tape involved a full month, even after which our movements throughout the country were circumscribed.

The reasons for such red tape are justified even if they are a complication to the potential field worker. Americans' interests in foreign lands do not always coincide with those of the host countries. Today the so-called third world is especially suspicious of our intentions following our involvement in Southeast Asia. Asians are more aware than we are of the role academicians play in American domestic and foreign policy. Our research and conclusions are not always as "irrelevant" and "unrelated" as a young undergraduate thinks. Field research reports become part of our cultural heritage and go into information storage banks, such as those maintained by the Central Intelligence Agency and the State Department. Indeed, every paper we have written and published on Nepal has been solicited quite overtly by the State Department. As one becomes experienced in anthropological field work one realizes his or her importance in shaping our future relations with foreign peoples and learns to define professional goals more exactly.

Nepal has never been conquered or colonized by a Western power. In the future, however, because of its strategic position between China and India, infiltration by overt or covert means is a real possibility. Just as in the nineteenth century Christian missionaries unconsciously prepared the way for "gunboat diplomacy," so in the twentieth century scholars often prepare the way for "political influence."

At the same time, Nepal recognizes its dependence on foreign aid and technological expertise. It is a landlocked country, devoid of industry and dependent on agriculture. Because of its steep mountains and monsoonal climate, transportation and communication present serious problems. Until the 1950s, Nepal had no roads passable to motor vehicles. (Even now, the usual means of transport in the hills is porter, and the most common means of communication is word-of-mouth.) In the 1950s, India built a motorable road from Nepal's capital, Kathmandu, to the border of India, followed by a Chinese-built road from Kathmandu to Tibet. While we pursued our field work, these two were the only such roads in Nepal. Recently, another was built connecting the Nepal and Pokhara Valleys in the western part of the country; and an east-west road in the southern Terai area is presently under construction and near completion.

Transportation and communication difficulties are compounded by high rates of illiteracy and a growing population, making Nepal economically underdeveloped and dependent on foreign powers for support.

7

Nepal therefore maintains an "open door" policy regarding research despite political dangers, relying on its careful screening procedures to minimize the risks. Anthropologists are still welcome but they must always bear in mind that a trip to Nepal might prove to be professionally unproductive.

In 1967, our project was rejected at first by the Nepal government, for reasons still unknown, probably because we had not published and were not established long in our field. After soliciting recommendations and conferring for weeks with other scholars and government officials in Nepal, however, we were granted a year's research visa. Looking back on our own experience, we would counsel the future researcher to amass plenty of letters and documents to justify research and establish credentials. Contacts with anyone who has worked, or completed research, in Nepal should be explored prior to a trip.

## Our Research Area

Eastern Nepal, the homeland of the Limbu people, includes six modern day administrative districts and an area of about 4,500 square miles. Pallo Kirat, or Far Kirat is another name for the area, and the Limbu and the neighboring Rai in Eastern Nepal are sometimes referred to collectively as Kirati. The Limbu call their homeland Limbuan, which is the term we use. Limbu have settled for the most part along the Tambar River and its tributaries and along the four rivers (Char Khola) in the Ilam district. Most Limbu recognize the far western areas of Pallo Kirat along the Arun River as the homeland of various Rai groups, especially the Yakha, Athapare, and Lahorang Rai, whom they refer to as their "brothers."

Historically, Limbuan is defined as ten indigenous provinces or "kingdoms" along the Tambar River and the four rivers of Ilam (see map). The names of these historic provinces, are well known to most present-day Limbu, and are cited when they wish to identify Limbu settlements. They are: Tambar Khola, Mewa Khola, Maiwa Khola, Yangarup, Panchthar, Phedap (including Atharai and Tehrathum), Chaubise, Mikluk, Chathar, and Char Khola (Ilam). All were still formally constituted administrative districts as late as the 1950s. The provinces correspond to the legendary founding of Limbuan by ten brothers who are believed to have migrated from Tibet and India, and subsequently to have established a confederacy of ten Limbu chiefdoms. Up to the middle of the eighteenth century, the Limbu maintained a semi-autonomous rule over these provinces.

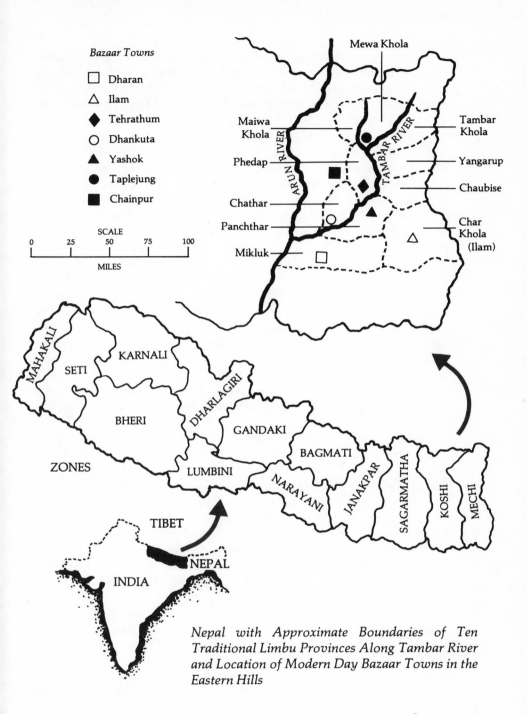

*Nepal with Approximate Boundaries of Ten Traditional Limbu Provinces Along Tambar River and Location of Modern Day Bazaar Towns in the Eastern Hills*

9

Limbuan encompasses the midland hill zone, the most fertile mountain zone in Nepal in climate and vegetation. The annual rainfall, mostly in the monsoon months of June, July, and August, can be as much as 175 to 200 inches. Elevations range from 1,500 to 12,000 feet in the midlands. Altitudes of 1,500 to 2,500 feet are generally uninhabitable because of steep slopes, rocky terrain, and a desert-like vegetation cover. From 2,500 to 5,000 feet the land is more fertile, the rainfall plentiful, and wet rice, the most important crop, can be cultivated. Between 5,000 and 8,000 feet, irrigated rice is seldom seen; instead, barley, maize, potatoes, soybeans, and other vegetables are grown. Altitudes above 8,000 feet are inhabited mostly by small numbers of Gurungs and Tibetan-speakers, who herd sheep and goats and also dry-land farm maize, barley, and potatoes.

The mountains of Limbuan are geologically young, with steep slopes, cascading streams and V-shaped valleys. Houses are scattered on the mountain slopes amid terraced fields and small forests. Compact village settlements with clearly defined boundaries are seldom found in eastern Nepal. Frequently, it is a day's journey to get from the top of one ridge to another, but at night in the silence one can often hear people laughing and talking on the other side of the valley, a half-day to a day's walk away.

Today, as a result of long-term Nepali immigration, Limbuan is a multi-ethnic society. The Limbu claim to be the original inhabitants, but they are no longer the most numerous. It is estimated that the Limbu comprise approximately 25 percent of the population of the ten indigenous provinces. High-caste Hindus (the "twice-born"), the Brahman and the Chetri, together make up an estimated 40 percent of the population. ("Twice-born" refers to those groups who undergo a ceremony and wear the "sacred thread" which signifies that they have been reborn into a higher caste. High-caste Hindus, Brahman and Chetri, in Nepal are of twice-born status: Limbu, and other middle-range groups, are not.)

Next are the various tribes who have adopted Nepali as their native language and have emigrated in recent years from elsewhere in Nepal— the Sunwar, Gurung, Magar, Rai, Tamang, and Tibetan-speakers. Together they comprise an estimated 20 percent of the whole. Of these, the Rai most resemble the Limbu culturally; they differ primarily in language (they usually speak only Nepali). The most numerous are the Tamang and Tibetan-speakers most of whom are Tibetan Buddhists and culturally quite distinct in dress, eating habits, and subsistence patterns. Tamang are scattered all over Limbuan, but the Tibetan groups, Sherpa and others, mostly occupy the northernmost fringes of Limbuan near the

Limbu houses and fields nestle against the
slopes of the Himalayas.

Himalayas. Magar, Gurung, and Sunwar in Limbuan have begun to
adopt the cultural patterns of the high-caste Hindus, except in name and
eating habits. Some of the most numerous and prosperous latecomers are
the Newar, emigrants from the Kathmandu valley who comprise about
10 percent of the population. The large bazaar centers of Dhankuta,
Chainpur, Taplejung and Tehrathum are inhabited mostly by Newar
shopkeepers, although many Newar groups have filtered into the
villages. Finally, around 5 percent of the Limbuan population are menial
or untouchable castes—tailors, blacksmiths, and leatherworkers.

In Limbuan, all castes and ethnic groups till the soil, including the
Upadhiya Brahman, who will not work in the fields in other countries.
The menial castes usually depend on crafts for their livelihood but will
also farm small plots of land.

*11*

## Reaching Our Village

We had chosen to begin our field work in the center of Limbuan, near the Tehrathum Bazaar, because we were aware of the work of Caplan in Ilam and Sagant near Taplejung, and hoped our work would eventually complement theirs.

One of the most physically demanding problems of field work was mobility. For example, it was very difficult to reach our chosen village. We were told we could either walk the 200 miles from Kathmandu a fifteen- to twenty-day journey, or take a shorter route by flying to a town on the Nepal/India border, Biratnagar, in a DC–3 aircraft, riding fifteen miles on a bus to the base of the foothills at Dharan Bazaar, and then walking the remaining fifty miles to Tehrathum. The latter way seemed best.

We arrived in Dharan Bazaar in November 1967, and hired three Limbu porters to transport our belongings. We had letters from several Limbu men in Kathmandu which would introduce us to their relatives in the hills. The porters estimated the journey at three to four days or, without the sixty- to eighty pound loads, two days.

By the end of the first day, exhausted from climbing steep trails and then descending in order to climb again, we were having trouble keeping up with the porters. In the end, it took us four full days to make the fifty-mile trip, with the porters waiting for us each step of the way. Hiking boots, which weighed us down and caused blisters on our feet, yielded to tennis shoes and rubber thongs for the remainder of our stay.

## Culture Shock

When we arrived in Nepal in the fall of 1967 we thought we were experts on the country and well prepared to meet all exigencies. But after a few months in the field, the romantic appeal of the mountains had faded and we began to experience that peculiar transformation of personality which anthropologists have labeled "culture shock." This phenomenon probably has a hundred different manifestations, but in our experience it seemed to affect the stomach first. The food in Limbuan seemed absolutely inedible. We dreamed of ice cream cones, ham and eggs for breakfast, roast beef for lunch, and steak for dinner. We lost weight rapidly. If the topic of conversation was not food, it was disease: "I think I have amoebic dysentery. No, maybe it's hepatitis." Rex once convinced himself he had tuberculosis and underwent two weeks of checkups in

12

Kathmandu, only to receive lab reports that were negative on all counts.

Interacting with the people became a chore, and often even the simplest conversation ended badly. On one occasion during this period, Rex was making small talk around the fire with a Nepali friend when suddenly the Nepali words were like incomprehensible gibberish. He ran outside the house into the fields, yelled at the top of his lungs, and then broke into tears.

Sometimes we found ourselves wondering why we were there. All the years of study and the research project did not seem reason enough. We concentrated on staying alive, and slept for fourteen hours at a stretch. We kept to ourselves. No longer "experts," we had difficulty performing the easiest task. Certainly the technological conveniences of our own culture, which are often scorned and taken for granted, seemed attractive at that point.

We gradually recovered and began to reach out to our neighbors. Slowly, we learned to respect *their* tastes, *their* likes and dislikes, and even began to adopt some of *their* ways. By the end of our field work a meal without rice was incomplete, and we appreciated why, in Nepali as in other Asian languages, the word for meal *is* "rice." The people we had thought of as sources of information became friends and surrogate relatives. We laughed, argued, got angry, and, frequently, cried with them. We began to understand that oft-repeated Nepali word *dukha* (hurt, suffering, misery) and also to see why the Limbu so often juxtaposed *dukha* with *sukha* (happiness) to describe any subject from the marriage of a daughter to a death in the family.

Our slow metamorphosis from culture shock to acceptance was a process as mysterious to us as our earlier descent into alienation. Maybe the cause lay in the realization that the people we came to study were not very different from ourselves, in spite of their unfamiliar lifestyle, tastes, values, norms, and beliefs. Perhaps this is after all the greatest value of anthropological field work and participant observation—this learning to question former "absolute truths." We would add also that humor served us well, and a healthy ability to laugh at oneself should be as much a part of an anthropologist's field kit as his notebook and research plan.

## "Nepali Time"

By the middle of our stay, we thought nothing of walking half a day to visit a friend. We also forgot our Western concepts of time and switched to "Nepali time," which can be summed up in a phrase that translates literally "tomorrow or the next" but really means "someday" or "sometime."

At first it was exasperating to make an appointment with a friend and have him not show up. Was this a sign that we were not wanted? No, we learned, it was just the Nepali custom. Later, if a Nepali undertook to meet us at a certain time, we would jokingly inquire whether it was "clock time" or "Nepali time." He would always laugh and say, "Nepali time," meaning he'd be there if and when it was possible to get there. If we were invited to a home for the mid-morning meal, we would ask, "What time?" The reply would be, "Nine o'clock." But, at nine, the family would be in the fields and only when they saw us did the tedious one- or two-hour preparation of the meal begin. They explained, "Why have the food prepared? What if you did not come, or came in the afternoon? We would be angry. Now that you are here, we can talk while the meal is in preparation, and we are all happy."


## Food Production

Without electricity and refrigeration, a Westerner learns to adjust his diet. We take supermarkets for granted, where we can buy almost any food we want all year round. In Nepal and elsewhere in the world, a fieldworker learns to eat seasonally.

The planting cycle of Limbuan is closely related to the growing season, the altitude, and the availability of water. At lower altitudes (2,000 to 4,000 feet) where there is water for irrigation, crops take less time to ripen but the growing season lasts year-round. Rice is the chief crop, followed by maize, wheat, barley, vegetables, and fruit. Sometimes two crops are planted in the same plot of land during the year. At altitudes of 4,000 to 6,000 feet, the growing season is much shorter (from April to November, or, if water is plentiful, to December), but crops take longer to ripen. Maize (corn) is the chief crop, followed by barley, soybeans, potatoes, rice, and a few vegetables such as string beans, tomatoes, squash, pumpkins, and cucumbers. At altitudes above 6,000 feet, maize, barley, potatoes and buckwheat are the chief crops. The growing season is short and the crops sometimes take six or seven months to ripen.

Nepali fields are either irrigated lands or dry lands. Irrigated lands are generally reserved for rice, or sometimes wheat. Vegetables are planted in the ridges which separate the terraced fields. Maize, barley, soybeans, and other vegetables are planted in dry lands at altitudes of 3,000 to 5,000 feet. Banana trees and other fruit trees are planted near the houses and gardens.

Maize is ordinarily planted after the first pre-monsoon thunderstorms in April, marking the beginning of the planting season, but in the lower altitudes maize is often planted in early March. The ground is broken by the plow, followed by women and children who broadcast the seeds. After the first hoeing, beans and squashes are planted at random in the dry lands among the maize stalks. The first weeding is done when the maize sprouts are four to six inches high, the second weeding just before the ears begin to sprout. Maize is harvested at lower altitudes in June or early July, at the mid-altitudes in August, and at high altitudes as late as October. The stalks are picked and fed to the animals. The heads of the stalks are stored on racks made of long, slender tree trunks suspended ten to twelve feet off the ground to prevent the grain from being eaten by rodents or other animals.

Rice, or paddy, is planted in seedbeds in May and transplanted to the irrigated lands in June or early July. The lands are prepared with fertilizer made of leaves or kitchen midden, plowed with teams of oxen, flooded, and smoothed by the oxen. Paddy is commonly harvested in October or November. The sheaves of grain are dried, brought to a hard flat area, and there threshed by pairs of yoked oxen. The grain is then stored in bamboo baskets, and the stalks are either fed to the animals or made into mats to be sold in the weekly markets. Paddy is often rotated in irrigated lands with wheat, which is planted in November and harvested in May to accommodate early crops of rice, harvested in August or September.

Potatoes are planted in dry lands at higher altitudes in December or January and harvested in March or April; in lower altitudes they may be planted in August and harvested in October or November. Barley, a dryland crop, is planted while the maize is ripening in July, first in seed beds and later transplanted, and harvested in October and November. Tomatoes are occasionally cultivated near the houses or along the edges of the fields. Mustard seed is also planted in July in the dry lands near houses and harvested in January. Soybeans are planted in the dry lands alongside the maize stalks, and are harvested in early September or late August. The plants are pulled out by the roots and brought to the courtyard in front of the house, where they are threshed with a stick to separate the kernels from the stems.

Oranges are plentiful from October to February, while bananas are picked at low altitudes year-round. Mangoes ripen in the summer months, during the monsoons, and many other fruits and berries, such as the jack-fruit, put in their appearance during the same months (July to September). Summer, a dreary rainy season, was brightened for us by the discovery of new tropical fruits at the weekly markets.

## Caste Dietary Restrictions

Every caste and ethnic group in Limbuan cultivates the soil in essentially the same way. Variations are determined by terrain, the availability of water, and soil quality. Although the Brahman and Chetri do not drink alcoholic beverages, they raise barley which they sell to brewers. Everyone in the hills of Limbuan raises livestock, but the breeds, and the purposes for which they are raised, differ.

All castes raise cattle and water buffalo if they can afford to. The animals are milked, and dairy products such as clarified butter and yogurt are consumed by everyone, particularly the Brahman and Chetri. Beef carrion is eaten by the leatherworkers, who remove the dead cattle. A few Tamang and Tibetan-speaking families eat beef as well, but killing a cow is forbidden by law. Water buffalo, especially bulls, are raised for meat as well as for dairy products; only the Brahman and Chetri refuse to eat water buffalo. Goats and chickens are also raised everywhere. Few Brahman families are strict vegetarians and most eat eggs, chicken, or goat. Goats are never milked but raised solely for their meat. Razor-backed pigs are raised by the Limbu, as well as by the menial castes, Tamang, Tibetan-speakers, and Rai—but not by the Limbuan Magar and Gurung or the Chetri, Brahman and Newar. The pig is extremely important to the Limbu. It is not only a staple in their diet and central to the blood sacrifice accompanying many of their household rituals; it also figures prominently in the marriage payments that follow the wedding ceremony. Sheep are seldom raised in the lower altitudes except in Ilam, but are kept by the Tibetan-speakers and Gurung in the highlands. Ducks and geese are raised primarily for eggs, and are eaten rarely by most castes.

A multi-ethnic society in which caste relationships and strata are signified by diet, creates problems for fieldworkers. We chose to stay with the Limbu diet as much as we could, and for this reason everyone accepted our craving for meat, especially pork. But meat was seldom available more than once a week, and, since there were no means for preservation of slaughtered animals, we gorged ourselves then. Because we had the money to purchase chicken and other meats any time, we could

*16*

have gone overboard in self-indulgence, but the supply of chickens would have been rapidly depleted and a premium would have been placed on other meat. We learned with difficulty to conform to a relatively small intake of animal protein and substitute huge quantities of rice.

## Weekly Markets

Subsistence farming is the norm, but the farmers of Limbuan are not able to produce everything they need. Foodstuffs and the products of specialized crafts are traded or sold in numerous markets throughout the eastern hills. Although there are three or four permanent market centers or bazaar towns that serve this region, the weekly or biweekly market, is most important. Every household is within two to four hours' walking distance of a weekly market. There, food products and varieties of goods are made accessible to people who would otherwise be forced to buy only in their own villages or make goods at home.

A weekly market takes place on Friday at Chainpur, Taplejung, Tehrathum, Yashok, Phidim and Ilam, and from Thursday through Friday at Dhankuta. The weekly markets in the bazaar towns are much larger than those in the villages because of the larger urban population and the availability of goods imported from India in shops run mostly by the Newar. At these weekly markets, the people of eastern Nepal are not only able to find foodstuffs produced in the hills, but also have access to cloth, tennis shoes, radio batteries, kerosene, aluminum cooking gear, flashlights, lanterns, cigarettes, pens, pencils, matches, paper, ink, sugar, salt, spices, tea, and jewelery. Even in remote hill villages far from the main trails, one encounters shops that sell those items, but only in the bazaar towns are the shops well stocked.

The weekly market provides the hill man with a holiday, a means for social intercourse with friends or distant relatives, and a chance to sell or barter. Even if he does not bring goods or foodstuffs to the market, or has no need to make a purchase there, it is still an opportunity to gossip, drink tea in the shops, or just sit around and watch the hustle and bustle. Here he learns the weekly news in the absence of newspapers or other local communication, and the current price of grains or other commodities.

A farmer usually comes to market with one or two items that he hopes to sell or exchange. A couple of chickens may be sold to buy a pig, or milk products may be exchanged for rice or maize. Cloth or basketry made at home may be sold to purchase food or pottery. Limbu women, especially, buy barley, and brew it into beer or distill it into liquor. The beer is sold near the weekly markets for a profit, which is retained as part of the women's personal wealth.

There is an abundance of foodstuffs, but most markets have smaller sections for the sale of pottery, cooking wares, steel and iron implements, brassware, basketry, village-woven cloth, wooden containers and leather goods. Fruits and vegetables, especially, are seasonal. During the monsoon from June to September, basketry and cloth are not featured since the hill man is too busy in the fields to produce them.

The market is laid out according to a plan which is not always adhered to by sellers. Animals are slaughtered on market day, and the meat is purchasable along the surrounding main roads. In the market proper, which is usually on flat land prominently situated near main trails or important shrines, are rows of people selling fruits, vegetables, and grains.

Ethnic and caste diversity in Limbuan is reflected in the arrangement of the weekly market. Goods manufactured and sold by the menial castes (blacksmiths, tailors, and leatherworkers) are located on the fringes of the bazaar, far from the edibles. Salt and tobacco, portered up from India by the poorer Limbu, Tamang, and Tibetan-speakers, are sold near the entrance areas. Food staples such as rice, millet, corn, and vegetables from the more profitable farms run by the Chetri, Brahman, and Newar, occupy the center area. Wealthy Newar traders who have shops in the bazaar towns set up temporary stalls, usually in the center of the bazaar, to sell pens, pencils, cigarettes, matches, and spices. Limbu women line up in another section to sell village-woven cloth.

The medium of exchange at the market is the Nepali rupee. Prices fluctuate in relation to supply and demand or the scarcity of goods (tempered somewhat by the idiosyncracies of the peasants), and are watched closely. People who have portered salt into the hills from Dharan Bazaar will sometimes hoard it for months, waiting for scarcity of the item to push up the price.

A vendor is often coerced into selling a scarce item at a low price by a buyer who intimidates the seller into meeting his offer. Kinship or long-established bonds of caste also influence market prices. For example, when clarified butter is at a premium during the dry season, people prefer to sell at cut-rate prices to relatives or long-established patrons in the bazaar towns, hoping for reciprocity in the future. Goods are also exchanged along established caste lines, similar to obligatory relationships in India. High-caste families repay menial castes—for instance, blacksmiths—in rice, maize, and soybeans rather than cash. Thus, although supply and demand determines price in the weekly market, personal relationships between buyer and seller often bypass economic fluctuations.

For us the weekly market was a godsend. It was not only the availability of fresh food and the chance to visit with friends that made us look forward to this day throughout the week. The market to us was like a carnival, and substituted for movies, television, picnics, and other forms of recreation that we knew in America. Also, since we did not have our own land to farm, we would probably have spent a great amount of time in a door-to-door search for food and other household needs were it not for the market.

## Religious Practices

As Westerners, we identify religion with organized churches or cults replete with dogma, ritual, and sectarianism. The Jews, Catholics, and Protestants of our world worship in separate buildings with well-defined sets of customs. Atheists and agnostics are distinct groups. Forms for jobs, insurance, or schools frequently have a blank asking the applicant to state his religion. We had always classified ourselves as "non-religious."

Nepalis, both the Limbu and the non-Limbu, were amazed when they inquired about our *dharma,* which we at first translated as "religion." We replied that we did not have any. To a Nepali this is unheard of. Why? *Dharma* in fact stands for "way of life;" so to reply that one is without *dharma* is to say that one is nonexistent. Even atheists have *dharma* by that definition.

We learned to respect and participate in the rites and ceremonies of the Limbu people. No one asked if we believed in a particular god or goddess, but to shun the rituals was to shun the Limbu way of life. In later discussions, many Limbu revealed a startling amount of skepticism and disbelief about the attributes of gods and goddesses. The exclamation would be, "How should we know? We have never seen them." Most Limbu were not interested in the existential reality of a spirit or deity, but rather in *this* world. Unexplained misfortunes and accidents were often described as the work of angry gods or spirits of the dead, but there was also much skepticism.

Consequently the Nepali are tolerant of others' beliefs or non-beliefs in the spirit world. But in this world, social duty pervades every action and asocial behavior is not tolerated. Violating the rules of caste behavior and dietary restriction would bring public blame against the transgressor. The Limbu and high-caste Hindus chastised us for allowing members of untouchable castes near our cooking area or inside our home. They unanimously voiced disapproval of our slovenly, egalitarian ways as a violation of religion. "Believe what you wish, but conform to our customs." "It is the untouchable's 'fate,' his *karma;* one has no control over that." Since they told us that if we broke their rules they would be unable to take food from us and normal social intercourse would be thwarted, we reluctantly conformed.

Religion in Limbuan varies widely, but it centers around the propitiation of local deities, spirits of the dead, and gods and goddesses of the Hindu pantheon. Limbu beliefs, rituals, and gods and goddesses differ considerably from those of Hinduism or Buddhism. The high god of the Limbu is Tagera Ningwaphuma ("Knowledge"). He is often identified as the Bhagavan of Hinduism, the "Supreme Body of Knowledge" or the "Creator of the World." He appears to man in the anthropomorphic incarnation of Yuma Sammang, or "Grandmother Spirit," to whom many rites and ceremonies are dedicated.

## Festivals

Although Limbuan religious festivals and ritual observances are localized, a few Nepali festivals are celebrated by everyone. Dasein, or Dashera, is the most important of the general celebrations. It lasts for ten days beginning at the new moon of the Nepali month of Asoj (September and October), and honors the goddess Durga, an avatar of Kali, often referred to as the Goddess of War. In Limbuan, there are designated sacrificial areas to Durga near the homesteads.

On the first day of Dasein, the head of a Limbu household or group of households plants maize for the festival in a dish made of leaves. The dish is left in a dark place while the kernels sprout. The following days are spent cleaning, painting, and repairing the homes and erecting swings and Ferris wheels. For the Chetri, Brahman and Newar, one significant day of the festival involves a community procession to a sacred place which honors the most important local god or goddess. The ninth day is the day of sacrifice: goats and water buffalo are decapitated at sacred stakes in the villages. A Brahman priest is summoned to draw sacred symbols around the stakes, which are decorated with shoots of the maize sown on the first day of Dasein. The animals are sacrificed and all spectators receive a *tika* (blessing of rice mixed with curd and applied to the forehead) from the priest and the oldest household member. The blessing recipients give the priest money for officiating at the sacrifice. The last day of Dasein is called *tika* day, when individuals visit various houses to receive a blessing from the elders. The Limbu drink huge quantities of beer and liquor, and eat generous portions of smoked pork, water buffalo or goat meat.

Although the festival of Dasein was a happy occasion for us and a welcome change of pace, it had its drawbacks. As special guests of the area, we were obliged to gorge ourselves on pork, liquor, and beer in many Limbu homes and to eat quantities of rice cooked in milk and butter in high-caste Hindu homes. One day during our last Dasein festival, we consumed multi-course meals at four different homes between 10 a.m. and 6 p.m. and still had three more homes to visit. Reeling and nauseous, we returned home after the fourth meal and vomited everything, hoping thereby to gain strength for our further commitments. But the damage was done: we found ourselves unable to move until the next day.

During the Dasein festival, many Limbu also celebrate a traditional harvest rite of their own that requires the sacrifice of a pig to the high goddess, Yuma Sammang. In addition, the Dasein festival marks the time when the Limbu make a series of marriage payments—meat, liquor, and other gifts—to a new bride's family (see chapter 3).

Dasein is followed by another important national festival called Tihar (in India, Dewali), which lasts five days, each day highlighting another object of worship. On the first day crows are worshipped by sprinkling rice or corn in the place where dishes are washed. On the second day dogs are worshipped, given blessings, and bedecked with flowers. On the third day cows are tied to stakes near the house and worshipped as Lakshmi, the goddess of wealth. Their necks draped with garlands of flowers, they are fed rice, and curd blessings are applied to their foreheads. On the fourth day oxen are worshipped, and in the evening children and menial castes travel house-to-house begging gifts of food and drink. The fifth and most important day of the Tihar festival centers around "worship of the younger brother." A person who has no younger brother, or a younger brother who has no older sister, must be adopted as a "godbrother" or "godsister." One Limbu told us that on other days of the year the dog, the crow, the cow, the ox, and the younger brother are all recipients of much abuse and insults. Hence the rationale for the festival: "It is only proper to set aside a time to honor them; that is what Tihar is all about." Throughout Tihar, people gather at the festival grounds and ride on the Ferris wheels or the swings. Gambling is popular, since Tihar is the only time during the year when games of chance are legal in Nepal. The Limbu spend many festival nights celebrating with flowing beer and liquor.

As ethnographers and visitors, we happily participated in these two great religious events. Nepalis of all ethnic groups welcomed us during this time, especially because we were also the official photographers of the community. Since we had early on established a policy of giving photographs to families who requested them at funerals, wakes, weddings, and other ritual occasions, few local ceremonies escaped our attention. Invariably a messenger would knock at our door with an invitation to come and take pictures of the event. Toward the end of our field work, as many as ten or fifteen people a day came to our home asking for pictures. We were so bombarded with requests that we had little time to do anything else, with the result that we became irritable and snappish. Once again, our use of an ethnographic "tool" had backfired.

## Western Hospitality

Our home also won fame as a liquor stop because we brewed our own beer and liquor and customarily offered it to guests. In fact, it was not unusual for travelers from three days' walk away to stop and ask, "Is this the home of the Sahib who gives out liquor and takes photographs?" Our reputation for hospitality had grown rapidly. In the long run, however, we think we were the prime beneficiaries of our own "generosity." Indeed, in retrospect it seems small payment for the ethnographic information we collected.

We also came to be known as "community doctors." After a few successful cures of infections, dysentery, and other ailments, word spread that we gave "good" medicine. We bathed sores, applied ointments and bandages, and dispensed pills on a daily basis. By the end of our stay, we reserved early morning for "office hours" for our patients. If a sore foot healed well, we gained a lifelong friend. It was extremely rewarding to watch a child recover from a case of dysentery or pinkeye; the parent's gratitude was payment enough.

## Limbu Shamans

Doctoring brought us into close contact with Limbu concepts of disease and with traditional Limbu priests and curers, whom anthropologists call "shamans." There are five types of Limbu shamans in the Phedap area: Yeba, Yema, Samba, Phedangma, and Mangba. The differences in their functions might seem as subtle to a non-Limbu as the differences between a preacher, a priest, a reverend, and a minister would seem to a Limbu. All five types of shamans officiate at cyclic rituals such as weddings, first rice-eating ceremonies, funerals, wakes, annual harvest rites, and periodic ceremonies for the welfare of a household. On these occasions it is up to the family involved to decide which shaman to summon.

Their dissimilarities of approach emerge more clearly in the diagnosis and curing of disease, and in the prevention of misfortune and calamity. The Yeba and Yema (the first is male, the second female), for example, are specialists in illnesses or misfortunes caused by the spirits of envy and jealousy or by witches. In their youth, Yeba and Yema receive the call, in the form of a sickness caused by the spirits of envy and jealousy and become possessed or "crazy." Other Yeba or Yema teach them control over these evil spirits and thus effect a cure. Apprenticeship lasts for years, as the novice learns to bring on trance states at will, and by means of the trance to communicate with the supernatural world, to ward off witches, and to diagnose and cure disease. In the course of their instruction the Yeba and Yema study rituals as well as mantras, spells, and chants. In addition, they are taught to make special costumes and to deal with the powers inherent in various medicines and fetishes such as a tiger's tooth, a dog's skull, or an antelope's horn. Eventually they become full-fledged shamans capable of the "magical flight" of a soul during a trance performance and the diagnosis and cure of disease.

The costumes of Yeba and Yema are symbolic. Supposedly they represent more than a reminder of Limbu mythological and ritualistic lore—the symbols are "real," just as disease, death, life, misfortune, happiness, fear, and prosperity are real. The most remarkable feature of the costumes is the headdress, which depicts flight. Bird feathers are selected with great care by the wearer to represent his ability to fly in spirit form to the land of the dead (the home of a fiery demon that eats the flesh of the dead), or to the abode of the gods and goddesses of the Limbu pantheon. Indeed, while wearing the headdress (simultaneously singing, reciting tribal myth, uttering spells and mantras, and dancing to the beat of a drum or brass plate), the shaman becomes a spirit. He is then endowed with the powers of spirits and capable of communication in their language.

The Yeba and Yema shamans are called "sorcerer," "one capable of performing evil magic," in Nepali. Many Limbu refer to them as witches (persons with innate powers of evil) since they "eat blood" during the ceremony for ridding a household of envy and jealousy. The Limbu say, "When the eyes of jealousy descend, one needs a Yeba."

Limbu legend claims that at the beginning of time, the high god of the universe created the first shaman and gave him the knowledge of the Mundhum, a collection of Limbu myths. This first shaman, called a Phedangma or Samba, was born at the creation of light and dropped from the sky into a body of water. By contrast, the Yeba or Yema came out of total darkenss, although like the first Phedangma the first Yeba came from the sky and were created by the high god. Phedangma is associated with good and Yeba with evil. The Phedangma performs rituals to the creator, and cures and heals disease by chanting from the myths. His trances allow him to "fly," but only through the words of his chants or through power from the myths. Both the Phedangma and the Samba are specialists in Limbu ritual and make offerings to the high gods and goddesses. Neither wears the full costume of the Yeba or Yema, but will occasionally wear garlands of beads and bells, and play drums. Phedangma and Samba preside over the killing of household pigs in honor of the high goddess, at weddings and funerals, and at annual harvest ceremonies.

All diseases in Limbuan are believed to have supernatural causes. Therefore, cures are designed to control or eradicate evil spirits, pacify angry gods or goddesses, and eliminate the powers of witchcraft and sorcery. Every shaman has an individual medicine bundle containing fetishes with special powers to aid him in his expeditions into the spirit world. Each shaman's kit of fetishes is distinct since each had a separate teacher.

We thought these traditional curers might be jealous of our growing reputation as doctors and healers, but their reaction was just the opposite. Limbu were familiar with Western medicine because of the British Gurkhas, and did not hesitate to use it in times of illness. Since the cause was "supernatural" and the symptoms were "natural," the shaman treated the cause and we treated the symptoms. Once, a shaman who was our friend asked us for Western medicine to cure his own child of dysentery.

## Division of Labor Between the Sexes

Although Limbu women experience a great deal of independence in economic and political activities, the division of labor between the sexes in many situations is sharply defined. Public violation of these norms and values, we discovered, is very embarrassing to the community. For example, only women are supposed to carry water. If a man hauls water, it signifies he is poor and/or lacks a family. Once, after an argument with our cook and housekeeper, Rex went to the fountain to fill the water jug for cooking. As he brought it back to the house, neighbor women ran out to meet him, insisting that they carry the jug because it was so degrading for a man to do women's work.

During planting, cultivating and harvesting, men, women, and children work side by side in the fields. At other times men work mostly at building, repairing roofs, erecting racks to store grain, making baskets, constructing frames for looms and pens for animals. Women serve as errand runners—carrying wood, bamboo, earth, rocks, water, and other materials needed by the men in construction or repair work. In cultivation, men prepare the earth and work with oxen teams; women supplement their work by using hoes to smooth out the earth, tidying up the field, repairing terraces, planting seed, and transplanting rice. Only men work with oxen. They also plant, but only after the work with the oxen teams is finished. Maintaining crops is a joint effort involving entire families.

Spinning and weaving cloth is traditionally Limbu women's occupation, and although men sometimes weave baskets, only women weave mats. Until recently a good rule of thumb was that the women's bailiwick included cloth and straw, while the men's was confined to bamboo. There are indications that this rule is changing, however. In a return trip by Rex in the fall of 1975, a young Limbu girl told him that today some Limbu men are learning to weave cloth. She cited the case of one young man in a nearby village who weaves more than the women of the village and reaps a sizable income from his labors. This case indicates a response to a growing need for outside income.

Within a home, cooking is women's work, but on the trail men do most of the cooking and claim that women tire too easily after long hiking. Women actually carry most of the load on the trail, especially if accompanied by infants. Men also help prepare food at festivals, when there is a large crowd to be fed.

Most of the routine work inside the home falls to the Limbu woman. It is she who cleans, cooks, and prepares the meals, cares for the young children, and often feeds and cares for the animals. In addition, it is she who keeps the home constantly furnished with water for drinking and cooking and, since cooking is done on wood fires, makes sure a ready supply of chopped wood is always available. During the dry season she is occupied with spinning, weaving, and cutting wood to be stored for

## Women at Work

*Lower Left:* Old woman with grandchild spins thread.
*Below:* Industrious young woman weaves cloth for sale.
*Above right:* Removing hull from rice is a time-consuming job for a Limbu woman. *Below right:* Aged mother watches as daughter weaves a reed mat.

*Above:* Mother and son plow a cornfield. *Below:* A Limbu woman sells potatoes at the *hāt bājar. Right above:* Women stop to chat as they fill their water jugs at the fountain. *Right below:* The whole family helps make clay pellets for a pellet bow.

28

the rest of the year. Odd jobs, such as making mustard-seed oil, polishing rice, husking grain, or distilling liquor for sale, are also done during this season. She is further occupied with intricate preparations for the numerous festivals and weddings which take place in these months.

Men meanwhile repair houses or make the implements for weaving—spinning wheels, looms, ropes. Many take odd jobs portering for the Newar-owned shops during the dry season. Others travel to the Terai near India to buy salt, cotton or thread for later sale in the weekly markets; few men find seasonal work in those regions.

We needed an experienced cook and housekeeper for the duration of our stay in Nepal. Preparing food on wood fires requires skill and takes time. Water must be carried to the home from centrally located springs and fountains in large clay pots or brass jugs. Women wait in long lines to fill their pots, especially in the dry season when many water sources are inoperative or work only in spurts. Floors are made of packed clay and must be smeared regularly with a mixture of clay, water, and cow dung to prevent dust and damage.

To establish closer contact with the people, we employed a Limbu woman whose husband was absent and who needed extra money to feed her two children. She lived in a house nearby, and came to work each day. She had never worked as a servant before, and although we paid her a high rate compared to that earned by other domestics in the hills, she resented her employment and argued with us about her duties and responsibilities. She was not a great cook, but later became one of our chief informants and one of the best contacts we had with other Limbu households. She helped us tremendously in learning the language, and traveled with us to weddings and other social occasions. When her husband returned to the hills she left us, but by then she and her children had become a part of our family. Even our quarrels took on the semblance of family spats.

Our cook frequently served as translator and interpreter. By the end of our field work, although we felt we had a good grasp of spoken Nepali, it was still difficult for us to comprehend many Nepalis' speech mannerisms. The cook had grown accustomed to speaking to us slowly, understood our accent and idiom, and paraphrased others' meanings to us and vice versa. As a linguist friend who had worked in South India once remarked, we had developed a "pidgin Nepali" (which our cook, and others, began to learn before we left).

It is understandable if we are skeptical toward other anthropologists who go into the field and "learn a language" in one or two years. There are certainly different levels of conversational ability, but speaking and being understood in a strange language requires years of practice and hard work. Perhaps one day an anthropological linguist will publish a book on "pidgin" dialects that have been developed by ethnographic fieldworkers.

## Borrowing and Lending

Shortly after we had set up housekeeping, we learned a valuable lesson about the give-and-take of hill life. There is a Nepali verb loosely translated "ask or demand" which expresses this reciprocity. If one needs a particular pot to cook a meal, the cry goes out, "Go next door and demand it!" This is the Nepali version of borrowing. It is no exaggeration that, by the time we left, half our household utensils were scattered in a dozen different houses and half the utensils in our house were someone else's. Our cook was adept at taking inventory and knew the whereabouts of every pot, basket, spoon, knife, or jug.

This widespread borrowing became irritating. When we needed a missing item we would be forced either to retrieve it from a neighbor's house or borrow another from someone else. Invariably the neighbor would be in the fields, or away. The cook enjoyed going for a borrowed item; it gave her a chance to spend most of the morning drinking beer, gossiping, and avoiding chores.

Borrowing did not stop with household utensils. Word got around rapidly that the Professors Jones were a ready source of extra cash. At one point, over three thousand of our rupees (about $300.) were on loan to over a dozen families. We always loaned interest-free, and for a while did not require security; but we soon learned to take gold or jewelry as collateral. We never lost money, but asking for security stopped the drain on our finances and made people think twice before asking for huge loans. At the end of our fieldwork, a stream of people came to our house to pay loans and retrieve deposits. Amazingly, we only lost a total of fifteen rupees, or about $1.50.

The most frustrating aspect of lending and borrowing was that the responsibility to retrieve an object was the lender's. The borrower might keep it indefinitely, except if he wanted another item or a large cash loan. Many times, a woman would come to our home with something she had borrowed months ago, praise us at length, and tell us what generous and wonderful people we were—then ask for a sizable cash loan.

Living in a caste society which had a history of land tug-of-wars and animosity between the Limbu and high-caste Hindus presented us with many dilemmas. When the Limbu found out we were sincerely interested in them they began trying to involve us in their disputes with Hindu creditors and landowners. Most Limbu land (see chapter 2) is mortgaged to high-caste Hindus to whom the Limbu are heavily in debt. Sometimes, they would use us to secure loans from their creditors and then threaten to transfer their mortgaged land to us. We avoided these confrontations as often as possible, but it was extremely difficult when the person concerned had earlier proven he was a good friend. We were acutely aware of the potential explosiveness of these situations, since they were rooted in hundreds of years of ethnic clashes and cultural differences between the Limbu and high-caste Hindus. Many times our ignorance saved us. We could always beg off from involvement by claiming we did not understand or that we could not communicate. Trouble would disintegrate when the Limbu and high-caste Hindus laughed together at our lack of knowledge.

# The Changing Society of Limbuan

# 2

For many Westerners, any mention of India conjures up visions of a rigid caste system characterized by harsh dietary restrictions and an absolute prohibition of the slaughter and consumption of beef. The serious student of south Asian culture discovers that in many areas where the caste system prevails it is not nearly as inflexible as some reports suggest. The ranking of castes is constantly changing, and the rules of food consumption are just as variable. In a village or town, members of a local caste may decide, either informally or formally, to alter diet and lifestyle and thus raise their status. In addition, there are probably millions of people in India and Nepal who eat beef and whose customs furthermore do not prohibit cow slaughter, although local public opinion and laws may prevent them from the act. Among these groups are the untouchable castes, Muslims, and many tribal groups who speak various languages and do not live as their Hindu neighbors do.

Another oversimplification about south Asian society still prevalent even among anthropologists is that women invariably occupy a subordinate position. Many writers fail to understand the dynamics of women's roles in the economy and in decision making processes. In Hindu caste society, it is true that tradition and custom delegate public responsibilities to men while women tend to maintenance of the home, care of children, and other domestic activities. The male head of the household is worshipped almost like a god, and folklore states that a wife should pay ritual deference to her husband and other male superiors such as elder brothers or uncles. Indeed, until the practice was abolished by the British in the nineteenth century, a "twice-born" Hindu widow was required to commit suicide at her husband's funeral by flinging herself on the burning funeral pyre.

In many parts of Nepal and India, high-caste Hindu society still conforms to the old ways. Divorce and remarriage of widows are prohibited on penalty of being outcaste. Tangible property such as land is controlled and inherited by males to the exclusion of women, and women are denied a voice in village and caste politics. In many remote villages, women are given second-class status despite modern national and regional laws that guarantee emancipation.

Limbu women, however, have never experienced the thoroughgoing subordination that was, and still is, the lot of some high-caste Hindu women. Limbu law and tradition have always permitted widow remarriage, divorce, a personal income, and even the inheritance of land, under certain conditions. Today, Limbu women enjoy far more mobility and independence than their Hindu counterparts. They converse freely with men in public and in many instances participate in important decisions concerning property disposition. Much of this freedom results from a chain of historical events that pitted high-caste Hindu against Limbu in a long struggle for land ownership and political control of the country.

## Land Struggles in Eastern Nepal

We learned to be extremely careful when discussing topics relating to land tenure with either the Limbu or high-caste Hindus. There had been bad feelings over property division between the two peoples for two hundred years in eastern Nepal.

In the early part of the eighteenth century, the present boundaries of Nepal included a number of relatively independent petty chiefdoms. This situation obtained until King Prythvi Narayan Shah of western Nepal, the ancestor of Nepal's present monarch, began a series of conquests that was to lead to the centralization of power and the formation of the present state of Nepal. His military campaign to take over Limbuan began in the 1760s and ended with the conclusion of a treaty with the Limbu chiefs in 1774. By the terms of that treaty, the Limbu agreed to the prohibition of cow slaughter and allowed the immigration of Hindu castes into their homeland. They in turn were allowed to keep ancient customs, govern

34

themselves as they always had, and maintain their traditional land rights.

During the nineteenth century, many changes resulted from heavy immigration and population growth. Hindu immigrants, especially the high-caste Brahman and Chetri, began to outnumber the indigenous Tibeto-Burman-speaking Limbu. Because of numerical superiority and the favoritism they enjoyed from the Hindu monarchy, high-caste Hindus gradually imposed many features of their way of life on the Limbu; and at the same time an erosion of long-established Limbu land rights began.

Two land tenure systems have existed in Limbuan during the past two hundred years—the *raikar* system, which applies largely to the Hindu immigrants, and the *kipat*, which concerns the indigenous Limbu. *Raikar* is a freehold tenure system, meaning that if an individual acquires ownership of a piece of land he may sell or rent it at will to any fellow citizen, but it cannot be sold or leased to a foreigner without the government's or the King's permission. Although *raikar* land can be owned by any citizen of Nepal regardless of ethnic or caste affiliation, few Limbu owned land under the *raikar* system until recently.

The *Kipat* system is a form of "communal" ownership. Land classified as *Kipat* ultimately belongs to the Limbu people and cannot be sold or alienated permanently to a non-Limbu, regardless of his caste or citizenship. Limbu who own *kipat* land may sell or transfer it only to other Limbu. This system is similar to that pertaining to land on American Indian reservations: that land, too, is governed by treaty and tribal or ethnic group affiliation.

Because of the land rights protection accorded them by the 1774 treaty, the Limbu were able to occupy a special position in Nepal in relation to other peoples. For many years they governed Hindu immigrants who settled on *kipat* land. Early in the nineteenth century, land in Limbuan was plentiful. Hindu immigrants had but to ask local Limbu headmen for a portion of land to cultivate and it would be leased to them on a long-term basis at a minimal fee. The headmen would collect taxes from the Limbu and non-Limbu within their jurisdiction, impose fines, settle disputes, and pass laws on immigrants who settled in their territory.

By the end of the nineteenth century, Hindu immigrants were becoming increasingly dissatisfied. They outnumbered the Limbu, had tilled the lands more efficiently and productively than the owners, and now desired outright ownership. The central government granted Hindu demands despite Limbu protests that the action violated established treaty rights. Much *kipat* land was converted to *raikar* tenure, and as a result Limbu headmen lost their jurisdiction.

Hindu immigrants continued to convert new lands into *raikar* tenure until 1901, when the Limbu threatened to revolt. The government then decided to uphold the 1774 treaty and decreed that further alienation of *kipat* lands to the non-Limbu would be prohibited. By this time, since many Limbu were heavily in debt to the Brahman and Chetri, they continued to lease lands to the Hindu on a long-term basis.

The system of long-term lease became very complex. The Limbu could not sell *kipat* land but continued to lease it through mortgage. It is estimated that 70 percent of all *kipat* land owned by Limbu families today is mortgaged to the non-Limbu. In turn the Limbu farm this mortgaged land in exchange for some of the crops. The Limbu, who supply the labor while the Brahman and Chetri supply the capital, have thus become tenants on their own land.

How did this situation come about? An example will illustrate. Suppose that a Limbu agrees to let a Brahman farm a plot of land for ninety-nine years for a thousand rupees. Legally, if the Limbu decides he wants his farm back, he has simply to return the thousand rupees to the Brahman and he regains his land although the Brahman is allowed to keep any crops growing on the land at the time of the transaction. In practice, however, few Limbu are able to exercise this right because they cannot amass the cash needed to pay off the mortgage. Instead, the mortgage is typically passed on to their sons and grandsons. Furthermore, the mortgage principal is increased each time the Limbu owner needs extra money for a wedding, a funeral, or other obligation. Frequently he borrows this money from his Brahman mortgagee and the loan is tacked on to the existing mortgage. Land that went for a thousand rupees in 1900 may now have an inflated mortgage principal of five or ten thousand rupees because of repeated loans over the generations.

Most Limbu today do not have enough land to maintain their families and are hopelessly in debt to high-caste Hindus. They are forced to turn to their creditors for political leadership rather than the traditional chief, who often finds himself in the same position of dependency.

The areas which the Limbu cultivate are for the most part less productive than those that are mortgaged or have been converted to *raikar.* As one Limbu expressed it, "Bhotia (Tibetan speakers) live in the highlands on the grass, the Chetri and Brahman live in the lowlands and cultivate rice, the Newar live in the bazaars and sell things, and the Limbu live on what is left." Although not an entirely accurate description, this reflects a common Limbu attitude of antagonism and hopelessness regarding their holdings.

## New Avenues of Income

The land struggle has forced many Limbu families to seek outside sources of income to maintain a minimal subsistence. Many Limbu males have entered service in the British Gurkhas as mercenary soldiers; others have become migrant laborers in the lowlands of Nepal and India, and sometimes emigrated there. Today thousands of Limbu families live in Sikkim and Assam in Darjeeling, Kalimpong; most of them emigrated there in the late nineteenth and early twentieth centuries. Those left in Limbuan supplement their livelihood through barter, sale of cloth and liquor, and wage labor.

To many present-day Limbu, military service in the British Gurkhas means escape from the pressures generated by growing population and diminishing natural resources in the hills, as well as extra income. During the nineteenth century, most recruitment by the British took place in western Nepal and the Kathmandu area, but at the turn of the century the Gurkhas began admitting Limbu and Rai from the eastern hills. The Limbu in particular responded to this opportunity. By the time India gained her independence in 1947, some 50 to 60 percent of all adult Limbu males had served in British Gurkha regiments; many fought in World Wars I and II in Europe and Africa as well as in Asia. Even today, most Limbu families can boast of a son or husband who has served in the British army.

Military service provided Limbu families with money to buy goods in Singapore, Hong Kong, and Europe for their families back home. Many chose instead to purchase gold, which they smuggled into Limbuan when they were furloughed or retired. Such hoarded assets, together with the pension payments received after retirement, enabled some of them to wipe out debts incurred to high-caste Hindus and to retrieve long-mortgaged lands.

Each year during January, pensions are paid at designated hill stations by a team of British officers. We had occasion to witness one of these annual distributions when we lived in Tehrathum. In fact, since the house we lived in was a pension-paying station, we had to move out when the officers came. Fortunately, we had made friends with the owner of a large tea shop across the street and were able to rent rooms for the ten-day period. Word had been spreading for months that the British officers would soon be coming. On the designated date, hundreds of Limbu descended upon the bazaar from miles around, ready to collect their pensions and celebrate. Local women made huge quantities of beer to sell day and night to the ex-soldiers and their friends and families. The new arrivals stayed with Limbu friends or relatives. Each night the hills resounded with the sounds of local girls and ex-soldiers dancing and celebrating.

Those who retired with a high rank received larger pensions. A few top-ranked officers realized enough cash from their military service not only to buy back mortgaged *kipat* lands but to invest in new property as well. A new elite class of retired army officers was thus created, many of whom became wealthier than their Hindu counterparts. They also began taking over mortgages, especially those incurred by Limbu relatives and held by Hindus. This select class became the focal point of social change in Limbuan, and gradually replaced the chiefs as leaders of their people.

Some Limbu families today who are unable to share in the benefits of military service earn extra cash through migrant labor in the lowlands of eastern Nepal and India. During the monsoon, men from families who have a surplus of laborers and do not cultivate lands for rice travel to the lowlands or India for a month and hire themselves out to Hindu families or other Limbu. In this way they earn enough cash to purchase scarce items such as salt, cotton, or processed thread, which they porter into their villages and sell in the weekly markets. Frequently they give the cotton and thread to their wives and sisters, who weave it into cloth to sell.

Petty trading ventures are another source of cash. One of the more lucrative is the purchase and sale of bristles from the hill variety of razorback pigs which nearly all Limbu raise. During the slack part of the agricultural cycle, some journey house-to-house bargaining for bristles to sell in the lowlands. With this cash, they may again invest in products to trade in the weekly markets near their homesteads.

Probably one-third of outside income, other than army service, comes from the sale of beer and liquor (Caplan 1970: 122, cf. Table 19). It is not an overstatement to say that every adult Limbu woman knows how to brew beer and distill liquor, and the vast majority sell both. Wood sold for domestic purposes, again mostly by women, is the next most important source of cash. Yeast used in making beer and liquor is sold only by women who have passed their childbearing years. Limbu women explain that making this "medicine" requires them to gather herbs from the forest, which might cause a young woman to become infertile.

*38*

The production and sale of village-woven cloth, straw mats, and baskets is profitable also. Of these activities, only basket-making can be said to be a male-run enterprise. The combined female commercial ventures involving liquor, wood, cloth, yeast, and mats account for over half the total cash income of Limbu families (Caplan 1970), including military service.

Caplan (1970:122), who worked in Ilam province, estimates that Limbu commercial activities provide money "equal to approximately 38 percent of net agricultural income." Supporting evidence is indicated for the northern provinces by Sagant's (1969) study of weekly markets. Although the majority of Limbu families probably realize less than half their income from commercial enterprises, a select few may earn as much as 90 percent of their income from nonagricultural sources. Most hill men earn their livelihood by farming supplemented by occasional trade, sales of village products, and hired labor.

## The Caste System

We have suggested how the idea of caste has been imposed on the Limbu by high-caste Hindus as a result of the struggle for land in eastern Nepal. Elite Hindus trace their status in the caste hierarchy from the old legal code of Nepal, which asserts that they alone may wear the sacred thread and be called "twice-born." Since their ritual purity is sanctioned by both law and tradition, they feel that privileges regarding land, wealth, power, and authority also are theirs by inherent right.

The laws that support these assumptions are alien to the Limbu. They tolerate Hindu attitudes with reluctance and only because of their own weakened position since the high-caste Hindus have "eaten" their land. Rules governing behavior between castes—dietary restrictions, the ritually pure status of the Brahman, the stigma attached to certain occupations, and patterns of avoidance and deference—are followed by the Limbu with extreme misgivings and latent hostility. In essence, they view the caste system as a foreign intrusion whose rules must be observed as a temporary expedient.

Brahman and Chetri define castes according to dietary laws, food consumption, and occupation. The castes so defined fall into three main categories: (1) the ritually pure or "twice-born" castes (Upadhiya Brahman, Jaisi Brahman, and Chetri); (2) the drinking castes (Rai, Gurung, Magar, Limbu, Tamang), ranked in various orders depending on the context; and (3) the menial or untouchable castes composed of tailors, blacksmiths, and leatherworkers.

Since all castes in the far eastern hills derive their livelihood primarily from farming, occupation as a criterion for ranking is largely irrelevant. The exceptions are the untouchables, who also perform traditional services for high-ranking castes. The Newar have their own internal order of ranking, but the Brahman and Chetri usually assign the Newar to the high-ranking drinking castes.

The Limbu see themselves as occupying a central position in the system, surrounded by groups who insist on certain forms of behavior and must be treated accordingly. A Limbu friend, slightly irritated at our incessant questions about the order of ranking, diagrammed the situation on the ground (Figure 1).

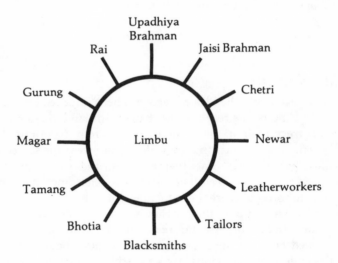

Figure 1

"In the center," he explained, "are the Limbu, because this is our land and our country. We are number one. We speak a language different from the others. On the outside are the other people because they are foreigners, they speak Nepali, and live here only because the Limbu invited them to. We accept water and cooked rice from the Brahman and Chetri because they are the same people as the King of Nepal; we do not accept water and cooked rice from blacksmiths, tailors, and leather-workers because it would be a sin; we accept cooked rice and water from the Rai, Gurung, and Magar because they are our brothers; the Newar are different from all the others—from some of them we accept cooked rice and water and from some we don't. This is our custom."

Not all Limbu would accept this man's description of caste differences, especially high-ranking Limbu who imitate their Brahman neighbors. Some Limbu will assert strongly that caste is a Brahman/Chetri concept with which they do not agree, and yet refuse to allow untouchables near their kitchens. Others might explain the most intricate details of avoidance, deference and food consumption with great clarity and apparent acceptance, and yet in practice violate the rules as if they didn't exist.

A number of Limbu said they would not accept cooked rice or water from the Tamang, who eat beef, but two Limbu brothers and one of the authors visited a Tamang blood-brother and everyone shared a meal of rice, vegetables, and beer cooked by the Tamang's wife. When we later confronted the Limbu brothers with the fact that they had violated the rules of food consumption, they vaguely rationalized, "He is a blood-brother," or, "It doesn't really make much difference with the Tamang."

Limbu adjustment to the caste system is subtle, intricate, and involved. In public, the Limbu validate the principles of caste relations, and for this reason Hindu concepts of inequality have been allowed to spread unchecked through the Limbu community. Pollution and purity concepts are accepted because the wealthiest and most powerful members of their community observe them, not because of tradition, history, or belief in the tenets of Hinduism.


## Differences between Limbu and Hindu Cultures

Limbu and Hindu cultures differ in many ways. Unlike other people in Nepal, such as the Magar of the western hills, the Limbu have not forsaken their own language and many resist learning any other. However, most speak both Limbu, a Tibeto-Burman language, and Nepali, the Indo-Aryan language of the Hindu immigrants. Wealthy Limbu who have succeeded in redeeming some *kipat* land tend to be fluent in Nepali and to speak it more than they do Limbu.

In Tehrathum, where we lived, the most influential Limbu was a retired Gurkha captain. He spoke Nepali even to the Limbu who spoke to him in their native tongue and frequently chastised those who insisted on conversing in Limbu: "We must learn Nepali if we are to better ourselves." This man's attitude may result in part from his military experience. A British major told us that Nepali is the only language allowed in the Gurkhas because, in the past, language was a source of conflict among soldiers from different areas of Nepal.

The lower a Limbu is on the economic scale, the less likely he is to speak Nepali. At this level, Nepali is considered to be the language of the Hindu conqueror and thus to be avoided except when communication is otherwise impossible. Limbu women, unless they are wealthy, speak Nepali less fluently than men. In Tehrathum and its environs, conversations among Limbu women were mostly in Limbu, while interactions with members of other castes and ethnic groups tended to be conducted in the crude hill Nepali that most women had to learn to conduct business in the bazaar and marketplace. The women of Tehrathum thought of the hill women who spoke no Nepali as backward and less sophisticated than they. During the pension-paying period, young Tehrathum girls pointed out groups of women dressed in homespun cloth as those who did not "even speak any Nepali." A few of these younger girls were even going to public school.

When the Limbu of wealth and rank converse among themselves, their own language is likely to be sprinkled with Nepali sentences and phrases. High-ranking Limbu rapidly lose their native vocabulary, especially words describing cultivation and commerce.

Dress is similar in basic design for the Limbu and the Hindu. Men wear cotton trousers, tight-fitting at the calf and loose at the thigh, topped by a tailored long-sleeved tunic which extends below the waist, overlaps in front, and is tied at the waist and under the arm with attached strips of cloth. Over the tunic is a waistcoat or a Western-cut suit jacket, accompanied by a small peaked cap. Women wear a sari, as in India, with a blouse tied almost like the men's tunic but extending only to the waist, accompanied by a shawl and jewelry of gold and silver.

Fashion differences appear in the choice of fabric and the ways in which the various articles of clothing are combined and secured. Limbu men of wealth, like high-caste Hindus, prefer trousers, tunic, and coat made of cloth imported from India or China, and a Western-cut coat. All apparel worn by the poorer Limbu is usually made of cloth woven by Limbu women. Wealthy Limbu women favor saris of silk or fine linen from India, and, unlike the poorer women, drape the sari over the shoulder. Lower-ranked Limbu women wear large strands of cloth tied over their saris at the waist like a cummerbund, and shawls of village-woven cloth. Impoverished women also prefer a blouse of black or red velvet, whereas high-caste Hindu women and high-ranking Limbu women ordinarily wear a cotton or linen blouse.

Both the Limbu and the Hindu have religious practices in common. Both worship a similar group of gods and goddesses, which vary in different areas of Limbuan. Both celebrate the principal Hindu holidays such as Dasein and Tihar, which honor Hindu goddesses (although Limbu recognize the non-Limbu derivation). Both acknowledge the sanctity of the cow, although the Limbu note that they ate beef before the conquest. Both accept the principles of certain forms of divination, especially that of rice, and both attribute illness and misfortune to supernatural causes such as "bad karma," witches, or the failure to propitiate mutual local deities.

The Limbu visit temples only on special local holidays but worship their deities at home or in the fields and forests, on grounds sanctified by Limbu shamans. Their rituals almost invariably call for a blood sacrifice, which Hindus in domestic worship avoid.

Nearly all Limbu families occasionally have Brahman priests cast horoscopes for newborns or read scriptures at a rite for the welfare of the household head. Conversely, high-caste Hindus frequently employ Limbu shamans to diagnose disease or perform simple acts of divination.

Lower-ranking Limbu commonly bury their dead rather than cremate them in the Hindu fashion, and a Limbu shaman is required to perform the funeral ceremony. High-ranking Limbu families, on the other hand, cremate their dead near a river and ask Brahman priests to perform the rites. They may even dispense with the traditional Limbu mourning ceremony, which takes place three days after the death of a woman and four days after the death of a man, and observe the Brahmanical pollution period of thirteen days after death instead.*

Most Limbu observe the Hindu rite of the first rice-eating ceremony for a six-month-old baby. Wealthy Limbu call on a Brahman priest to perform the ritual, while poorer families hold a simple ceremony at home without a priest. Instead, the head of the household conducts a short ritual with a few invited guests who offer money and give the infant his or her first bites of rice and solid food.

The marriage practices of the Limbu differ from those of the high-caste Hindus. The Limbu are married in the home of the bridegroom's family. Rather than a dowry, they require a brideprice (see chapter 3) as

---

*This observance requires that for thirteen days all members of the deceased's extended family must refrain from eating foods cooked in salt or oil, and must furthermore avoid social intercourse with non-relatives.

well as a series of payments after the wedding, made by the bridegroom's family to the bride's. Limbu shamans perform the wedding rituals which are accompanied by a blood sacrifice and large feast paid for by the bridegroom's family. Hindu weddings are conducted by Brahman priests in the bride's home without blood sacrifice. The Limbu accept widow remarriage and divorce, whereas those practices are forbidden by Hindu custom.

The Brahmanical pattern of marriage has not yet been adopted in Limbu custom even among the more wealthy Limbu, although a few Hindu cultural practices are evident in the wedding ritual. For example, the tailor caste is invited to all Limbu weddings to give blessings to the married couple, to sew the wedding garments, and to serve as musicians. In addition, the wedding garments of the Limbu bridegroom have taken on a distinctive Hindu flavor, and the umbrella that shelters the bridegroom and bride is a Hindu custom.

In the preparation of food, the Brahman and Chetri use a special cooking stove that stands on a platform made of mud and stone. The Limbu usually cook over a small depression in the floor with the cooking vessels supported by three rocks or an iron tripod.

The poorer Limbu seldom drink tea, which they call "the drink of the Brahman," and almost never have it in the home. The more wealthy Limbu keep a supply for visitors and frequent the tea shops during holidays, festivals, or weekly markets, while their poorer brethren look for a home where they might purchase beer or liquor.

Diet preferences are probably the most noticeable differences between the Limbu and high-caste Hindus. Many Brahman are strict vegetarians; the Chetri eat chicken and goat, but no other meats; the Brahman and Chetri avoid drinking alcoholic beverages. The Limbu eat chicken, goat, water buffalo, and pigs; and beer and liquor are an integral part of their lifestyle. The Limbu do not eat beef nowadays but are aware that their ancestors did.

A few wealthy Limbu families are edging toward adopting Brahmanical practices regarding diet. They have curbed their drinking habits and are reluctant to drink at all in public. The only Limbu who ever refused liquor in our home were high-ranking ones—and they said no because they had an important engagement with a government official or a high-caste Hindu. A few high-ranking Limbu are restricting their intake of pork as well, and some are eating only chicken or goat.

Diet is always the center of discussion when the Limbu talk about intercaste relations. Many feel guilty that they do not live up to Brahman-

44

ical standards in the foods they eat and so rationalize their poverty. "Why are the Brahman and Chetri richer than the Limbu?" "Because the Limbu eat meat and drink too much."

## Limbu Nationalism

Land struggles have created a strong Limbu nationalism which is often carried to the extreme by all classes. They unite in their response to disparagements of the *kipat* land tenure system and recent attempts by the Nepali government at land reform. Even though the poorer Limbu may not immediately benefit from lands they own in name only, they cherish the hope of regaining control of those lands in the future. The wealthier Limbu, of course, resist land reform because it will reduce the holdings which ensure their wealth and status.

By the 1930s, Limbu political deprivation and the land struggle had given rise to a religious cult led by an illiterate ex-Gurkha soldier who claimed to be the reincarnation of the Limbu high goddess and called himself Phalgunanda. The movement he founded, called the Satya Hangma or "Queen of Truth," amassed over five hundred followers. It advocated a return to old Limbu religious customs, and Phalgunanda urged his disciples to speak only Limbu. He claimed that if the Limbu followed his teachings they would regain all *kipat* lands and evict the Hindu immigrants from Limbuan. The movement gained ground in the 1940s when central government attempts to make surveys of land holdings in Limbuan aroused popular fears that the *kipat* was about to be abolished. When Phalgunanda died in 1946, the Satya Hangma movement dwindled. Satya Hangma still lives on in Limbuan, but as a religious sect devoid of political overtones.

The Satya Hangma movement represents a curious response to Hindu immigration and dramatizes the nature of Limbu nationalism. Members of the cult today will neither eat meat nor drink liquor, rules which clearly are not anti-Hindu in nature and do not represent a return to the Limbu way. Instead, they demonstrate the depth to which Hindu ideology has penetrated Limbu customs. Indeed, Phalgunanda himself felt that Limbu marriage practices contributed to economic and political deprivation owing to the high costs they exacted for weddings, bridewealth, widow remarriage, and divorce. He tried to force his followers to adopt the practices of the high-caste Hindus.

Many Limbu turned away from the Satya Hangma for these reasons. Our neighbors had heard of the teachings of Phalgunanda but thought his ideas were too radical. They did, however, agree with his politics, which were basically pro-*kipat*. Few Limbu women were attracted to the movement because of his advocacy of Hindu customs of marriage.

## Extended Effects of Social Upheaval

The changes that have occurred in Limbu society as a result of two hundred years of Hindu immigration and, ultimately, domination have been pervasive. We have seen how the Limbu had to accept new economic patterns and live with the attempts to abolish the communal land tenure system of *kipat*. The most extensive consequences for the society have been land shortages and an attendant transition to a cash economy. The Limbu had traditional exchange systems but are now obliged to place money value on goods and services. Even land, the most cherished of commodities, has assumed a cash value.

The Limbu were not altogether unfamiliar with money prior to the Nepal conquest. There are indications (Chemjong 1967) that for hundreds of years they had dealt with the powerful Tibetan kingdom of the north and the Hindu kingdoms of the south, all based on market economics and money or similar mediums of exchange. But for the most part they remained on the periphery of these political and economic systems and did little more than pay lip service to them even when threatened or conquered. They went about their daily lives relatively isolated from the rest of the world and depended on a subsistence economy to supply their basic needs. Almost the only product not locally produced was salt, which came from Tibet. The Limbu may have occasionally acted as middlemen for goods imported from India to Tibet, but little information is available on this subject. They probably produced some surplus grain such as rice, maize, or barley (used by Tibetans in brewing beer) to trade with Tibet.

The Hindu conquest of the eighteenth century was not like the others. From that time forward the Limbu, no matter how much autonomy they retained, became a part of a larger political and economic system. As the Hindu immigrated into their homeland a multiethnic community took shape, and the economic change that accompanied the progressive loss of land through sale and mortgage brought profound social change as well.

*46*

As the Limbu turned to the outside world for new sources of income, especially to military service, the family structure was altered. Because so many Limbu men were now absent from home for long periods, many of them as long as ten to fifteen years, much of the day-to-day decision making fell to the women. Many Limbu homes had no adult males, and so women did *all* the decision-making—when to plant, when to harvest, when to perform important household rituals. They made decisions about the marriages of their sons and daughters, handled the business affairs of their husbands' *kipat* lands, collected and paid taxes or interest on loans, even mortgaged *kipat* land in time of need. They took to the fields to perform many of the tasks once allotted to men—the planting, the cultivating, the harvesting—until in time the hoe even became known as "the woman's tool."

Men's long-term absenteeism and the assumption of new responsibility and decision making by women fostered a more independent-minded woman and drastically revised the marriage process. Documents from the early nineteenth century that concern Limbu marriage describe a complex ceremony performed by a Limbu priest, in which the bridegroom and his patrilineal relatives paid homage to the bride and her family through a series of marriage payments. Marriages were arranged between patrilineal kin groups headed by a chief who was paid to recognize the legality of the union. Negotiations between the families of the bride and groom were carried out through a mediator, usually a close male relative of the bridegroom. After negotiations and the wedding ceremony were concluded, the bride relinquished her family name on payment of a fee, and assumed her husband's family name. The whole marriage process was accomplished probably in a few days or weeks.

It is highly unlikely that in those times either the bride or the bridegroom had much to do with the marriage arrangements, bridewealth payments, or ceremonial gift exchanges. After the ceremony, the bride took up residence in her husband's household under the watchful eye of her mother-in-law and assumed her duties in subservience to her husband and his relatives.

Limbu men and women today exercise a greater degree of freedom in choosing a spouse. They court one another prior to marriage in a ritual dance discussed in chapter 4. Both partners take part in the marriage arrangements and the negotiations over bridewealth, and both are free to dissolve the marriage if they find it unsuitable. The marriage itself is no longer concluded with the wedding ceremony, but rather extends over many years through annual gift-giving and a final payment that sometimes does not occur until late in life, after the birth of children.

What is more, a woman nowadays does not automatically take up residence in her husband's household after the wedding ceremony. Her change of residence is a gradual process, and she often waits until after the birth of her first child. Close contact with her natal home is maintained even into old age, and her family name is not transferred to her husband's until the final marriage payment, sometimes ten or fifteen years after marriage or perhaps not until death.

All of this bespeaks a vast change since the time when Limbu men bore sole responsibility for the defense of their homes and lands and, according to old Limbu literature, all the sons in a family had to learn archery at the age of twelve. When men were seldom absent from the home for long, women were probably not concerned with politics, war, or diplomacy, traditionally male affairs in small-scale Asian agricultural societies. Myths surrounding the origin of the first council of mankind and the Limbu system of writing describe legal, religious, and literary practices as the work of men.

It is clear that the stereotype of South Asian women does not apply to the Limbu women of today who have begun to assume full political and economic responsibilities once assigned to men. Also, the caste system found in many parts of India and Nepal is altogether different in Limbu society because of the nationalism resulting from the Hindu conquest.

# Family Life and Marriage

# 3

The long history of conflict over land and the subsequent impoverishment of many Limbu families due to debts, high interest rates, and mortgaged property has affected the organization of the family, marriage, and the roles of Limbu men and women.

As an example, the woman we employed as a cook and housekeeper lived in a small house near the Tehrathum bazaar with her five-year-old son and eight-year-old daughter, while her husband had been in Assam for six years farming land with his brother and mother. Adjacent to her home lived a mother and daughter, both married but neither living with her husband. The daughter was nursing a baby girl. The two households worked together farming a few plots because most of their husbands' *kipat* land was mortgaged to a nearby Chetri family. But most of their subsistence came from wage work, the sale of beer and liquor, and sporadic income from one husband who had a government job in Ilam.

Female-dominated households are not unusual in Limbuan, and there are many young married women whose husbands are away or who have not yet moved to their husband's household. These women assume much of the work load and decision making even when their husbands are at home.

When Rex returned to the area in the fall of 1975 he conducted a survey of eighty-six women in three Limbu villages. The survey included all the married women of those villages. Over 20 percent of the households surveyed were dominated by females, many of them widows or women whose husbands were in the army or living in India.

Every Limbu married couple's goal is to own and live in their own home. Unlike Hindu families, few Limbu choose extended family households which include grandparents or married siblings. Couples cherish their independence and, after marriage and the birth of children, are eager to move away from their parents. Consequently, a "nuclear family household" is not uncommon and seems to be regarded as the ideal situation. The nuclear family household includes a husband and wife, their unmarried children, and occasionally a widowed parent, a sibling, or a young girl who is married but has not moved into her husband's home.

However, a young married couple would never abandon the older generation. Elders are respected and their advice and opinions carefully weighed and acted upon. Even men and women too old to work or be productive members of the community are cared for.

## Lines of Descent and Inheritance

Although a Limbu family may in many respects resemble an American family, it is connected to other families by descent, marriage, and ownership of property ties that are unfamiliar to us. The Limbu family has a strong patrilineal bias and, after marriage, the place of residence is limited because the man and wife try to live where they will inherit arable land. Because *kipat* land is passed from father to son in the patriline, a newly married couple often lives first in the groom's father's household. If possible, they live separately but nearby, on the portion of land to be inherited. Only rarely does a couple reside with the wife's parents or in their vicinity.

Equally uncommon are cases of two married brothers and their families living in the same household and farming a joint inheritance, as Hindu families throughout Nepal and India typically do. Ordinarily, two houses share a common courtyard for weaving, spinning, and winnowing grain. Face-to-face houses are customarily owned by two brothers, or a man and his married son, and function as one unit, particularly if the family has failed to divide its *kipat* land inheritance.

Near our town, two brothers occupied different levels of the same house for economic reasons, maintained separate family budgets and held separate household rituals, but cultivated undivided *kipat* land holdings. The oldest brother was employed elsewhere in government service, had two wives, and was often accompanied on his job by his second wife. His first wife and her two daughters occupied the upper level, while the childless younger brother and his wife lived in the lower level. Splitting the homestead into separate dwellings would have been inefficient and costly. The oldest brother's absence allowed room enough for both families, and it was safer for the oldest brother's wife and his unmarried daughters to live in a household with a male occupant. The household operated as two interdependent halves rather than one whole.

Exceptions to household independence depend on the nature of land inheritance and the domestic cycle (birth, marriage, and death within a given household) in Limbu society. *Kipat* land is inherited equally among sons, but in the absence of heirs, two or more brothers (as in the example above) often decide not to divide their holdings. Among the Limbu the subdivision of lands among sons does not depend upon the death of the father, as it does in high-caste Hindu society. Sons may demand their inheritance after they have passed puberty and are willing to cultivate the land themselves. The process of land division is however contingent upon the son's marriage and his willingness to sacrifice a possibly greater inheritance when his father dies, since he will have no claim to property accumulated later by his father's household. In practice, the partition of households and the subdivision of lands tends to be deferred until after potential heirs have not only married but produced children, preferably sons.

Households sometimes split because of quarrels between in-marrying females and a husband's married sister (or sisters) who has not yet moved permanently into her husband's household. A man's new wife and his mother may not get along, and if households are not partitioned the wife may soon return to her natal home and eventually "divorce" her husband through adultery.

Only sons who can establish lines of descent in the patriline are entitled to an inheritance. An illegitimate son may live on his mother's brother's land and cultivate it under mortgage or for a share in the harvest, but he is still an "outcaste" in Limbu society since he has no one to observe his funeral rites.

Sons of divorced women generally are entitled to an inheritance only in their father's household, although there are exceptions. For instance, in one case a man had "stolen" his first wife from another clan, but the woman was pregnant by her first husband. When the child was born he was raised in the foster father's household. When he reached marriageable age, he moved with his natural father but was unable to establish a good relationship. Eventually he returned to his foster father's home, married, and was given land to farm. His share was considerably less than his foster brother's, but he did receive an inheritance with his foster brother's consent. The boy, now about twenty years old, is hesitant when asked his clan name, sometimes replying one name, sometimes the other. Although it is against the rule of Limbu inheritance, the boy's attachment to his foster father in this case seems to have prevailed. Limbus claim this young man has no legal rights to the *kipat* of the foster father since his place is in the real father's household, and the foster brother could make him leave.

Women are allowed to inherit land only if they do not marry and leave the household and only if they are thirty-five years old or older. Even then, a sister is entitled to only half the inheritance of her brothers. If a woman decides to remain a spinster in her father's household, her land reverts to her closest male relatives at her death. If a woman marries first and then, through divorce or widowhood, returns to her natal home to assume an inheritance, she cannot hand the land down to her descendants.

A twenty-two year old girl of our acquaintance declared her intention to remain in her father's house and farm his land with her brother. But by the conclusion of our field work there were already indications that she might marry. Since most women hope to become wives and mothers, their inheritances seldom materialize. However, a woman has close ties with her natal kin group, and if she cannot establish harmonious relations in her husband's household she may always return to the house of her father or brothers. A widow is entitled to enough of her dead husband's land to maintain herself and her household. At her death, the properties pass to her sons or, in the absence of heirs, revert to her husband's brothers for redistribution.

A man's titles are inherited by his eldest son, or, in the absence of sons, by his next oldest brother and *his* sons. If a man has two wives, the eldest son of his first wife inherits the titles. The house itself goes to a man's youngest son, who will probably be the last to build a home of his own.

Because of the character of land inheritance, Limbus have a strong desire to produce sons. Families without sons many times adopt them or encourage young men to marry their daughters by promising cultivable land. A neighbor jokingly asked Rex to marry one of his daughters with assurance of land to settle on, since the neighbor had no sons as heirs. Many times a sister's sons are encouraged to take up residence on land with promises of succession, and in these ways patrilineal inheritance is often bypassed.

Livestock or household utensils are also inherited in the patriline, except the property that an in-marrying woman has or acquires after marriage. That land may be given to her daughters or other close relatives, is not automatically inherited by her sons, and does not become common property. The ownership and control of personal property gives Limbu women much greater independence than high-caste Hindu women.

## Lineages and Clans

The Limbu express the line of patrilineal descent as relationship "by the bone." Families related "by the bone" are grouped into lineages and clans. A lineage is a group of close-knit families who are descended from a common male ancestor. Most are "corporations" headed by a chief who is responsible for paying all their taxes.

The families in a lineage share a common bond when one of their lineage members dies, for the death of any one brings pollution on all the others. Ritual pollution is observed for four days after the death of a man and three days after a woman dies, during which time all adult members must not eat foods cooked in salt and oil. Members who are genealogically distant from the deceased frequently violate this rule in private, however. When an old man who lived near us died, the members of his lineage wanted to observe lineage pollution. His lineage included the descendants of the older and younger wives of his grandfather, and lived in two residential clusters separated by about an hour's walk. Shortly after his death, several women from the farthest residential cluster ate a snack which we had cooked in oil. We asked about the pollution violation, but they rationalized that it was all right because the old man was not their own grandfather.

The closest living male relatives of the deceased must observe a strict fast and may not appear in public until the pollution period is over. They must sit in a corner of the deceased's house clad only in white cotton garments, are allowed to speak only to lineage males, should not eat meat, and must drink only water. At the end of the pollution period the principal mourners give a feast for those who assisted in the funeral and burial, and they are then allowed to resume eating foods cooked in salt and oil.

The conclusion of the pollution period is also marked by a second, more important ceremony that signifies a return to normal social intercourse. Between the death and the second ceremony, lineage members experience a "social death"; that is, they may neither contract marriages nor hold other religious ceremonies in their homes. A second feast is then given by the principal male mourners, who must shave their bodies and offer ritual food and drink to the spirit of the deceased. The ceremony is attended by the members of the lineage, close neighbors, friends, and affines.

The second ceremony affirms the significance of marriage ties within the lineage. Wives of lineage males are accepted as full-fledged members only after the final marriage payment transfers the woman's natal family name to her husband's. Without the final payment, a woman's death is not considered ritually polluting to her husband's lineage. If death occurs before the payment is made, the husband will make every effort to present the money to her father and mother before the second ceremony is held. In the Tehrathum area, the payment is sometimes sent with the invitation. If a married woman dies, her mother, father, and natal kinsmen must be invited to attend the second ceremony. Affinal consent is mandatory to remove pollution from the lineage.

Rules of lineage pollution extend to the sharing of food, especially cooked rice and water. No Limbu will touch food or drink that has touched another person's lips unless it has been washed with fresh water. On the trail, when only one drinking vessel was available, each person would carefully pour water, beer, or liquor into his mouth without allowing the drinking vessel to touch his lips. Only lineage members whose pollution is shared escape this rule (*jutho milcha*, or literally "pollution mixes"). Males will not touch impure food of lineage females younger than they, nor will they take impure food from their wives. Wives absorb the impurities of their husbands, as well as other male members of the lineage in that they will eat leftovers from these men's meals.

Today, the lineage plays a small but not insignificant role in marriages. A nominal marriage payment should be made to the chief of the bride's lineage—as a recognition of the legality of the proceedings. The payment is often described as a "tax" on the lineage of the suitor for the legalization of the progeny of the woman whose children will be members of her husband's lineage. Today the payment is primarily symbolic because the authority of the headman over his lineage members has been lessened by directives from the central government. Also, the chief plays a role in the divorce proceedings of his lineage, acts as a mediator in disputes, and is given a few rupees for his services. The lineage must also observe pollution rites when women who have married into the group die.

The recognition of relationship "by the bone," or patrilineal descent, goes far beyond the lineage, since each lineage is part of a clan whose members claim descent from a common distant ancestor (whose name more often than not has been forgotten). Few people are able to trace a genealogical connection to the founding ancestor of their clan, while the connection to the lineage ancestor is generally known.

People who make up a clan share a common name and live near one another. The clan is not a ritual group, nor do its members observe pollution rites when a member dies unless the member also belonged to the same lineage. Men and women who share the same clan name are forbidden to marry or have sexual relations. Limbu legend tells of the marriage of a couple long ago who belonged to the same clan. One day while the woman was weaving, a thunderbolt crashed to the ground, and out came a pig that trampled the incestuous couple. Limbus still claim that this supernatural penalty will happen to couples who commit clan incest.

Marriage is also forbidden between couples who trace their descent within four generations of their mothers' clan. In one verified case, a man of the Tumbahangphe clan in Tehrathum married a girl of the Laoti clan in Panchthar. Since the couple were descended from the same maternal grandmother, public opinion and gossip forced them to leave the hills.

Members of a clan have certain rights to *kipat* lands which belong to other clansmen. If some lineages were to die out, their lands would revert to others within the clan. In this way, the clan maintains "continuity of possession" of *kipat* lands. Consequently, the Limbu do not have to stay in the area of their clan's *kipat* holdings to maintain ownership. They may be absent their entire lives and still retain possession, and they are not required to have been born on the land. They must, however, be able to trace a patrilineal connection "by the bone" to a past owner.

The clan's reversionary rights to lands do not extend to Limbu lands that have been converted or purchased under freehold tenure, or *raikar*. This property is held individually, and, in the absence of a direct heir, the recipient must be specified. The lands may be transferred to members of Limbu or non-Limbu clans.

Limbu family ties thus extend beyond the immediate family and are important in land ownership and control, the regulation of marriage, and selecting a spouse. Closely related families and lineages conduct death rituals together.

The lineage is also the primary political force in Limbuan. Unlike the inhabitants of other parts of Nepal and India, the Limbu do not live in compact self-governing villages. Until recently, when the central government divided the country into village councils, headmen and councils of old men within the lineage ruled. They still make important decisions and settle disputes, but the new system of courts and village councils is taking over.

## The Household as a Center of Ritual

The Limbu household refers to the building as well as the family that occupies it. The Limbu family is independent, economically and ritually. Except for marriages, deaths, or the Nepali festivals of Dasein and Tihar, all other ceremonies are held in, and paid for by, the household. Costs are minimal and include the preparation of food and beer for the shaman, paying for his services in cash or clothing, and procuring animals, usually chickens, for the sacrifice. Weddings and mourning rituals, however, can be very expensive, as we will see.

Each year, the members of a Limbu household kill at least one piglet from a new litter as a sacrifice to the Limbu high goddess Yuma Sammang. The pig must be domestic, and not bought specifically to be slaughtered for meat. A shaman is called to the household to perform the sacrifice and kill the pig.

A harvest ritual is celebrated in October or November after the barley and rice harvest, often by two or more households which have not divided their land holdings. The simple ceremony is similar to the pig sacrifice except that a cock is used. The harvest ritual is sometimes combined with a ceremony for the welfare of the family members. This rite is a form of divination of the chicken's entrails, whereby the shaman determines if the household will experience good or bad fortune in the coming year.

At least once a year, each male household head must go through a ritual for the good of his soul. At one we attended, a bamboo altar was erected in the corner of the main living area near the ceiling; on it were a vase of flowers, an offering of rice, an oil lamp, and one silver Indian rupee. The man's pellet bow, his bush knife, and incense were placed on the floor beneath the altar. A shaman began to chant in front, calling to God. He claimed he was conveying the man's soul to the high god's abode to assure future good health. The shaman and the household head periodically grabbed the bow and the knife and fought symbolically with the demons of misfortune and ill health. The ceremony ended with a cock sacrifice to Yuma Sammang and offerings to other important Limbu deities. As a final step, the cock was prepared for cooking. The wife took special precautions to see that every scrap was either eaten or destroyed,

*56*

## Women in Ritual

*Above:* During the festival of Tihar women make strings of flowers to decorate houses, people, dogs, and cows. *Left:* A Limbu woman makes an offering to her household deities.

57

since leftover parts outside the house might nullify the whole proceedings. She carefully burned the feathers and entrails, and served the cooked chicken with rice, warning us to eat every bite, even the bones, or else throw them into the fire.

The head of a Limbu household also observes the annual Hindu ceremony of thanksgiving to the god Satya Narayan for a bountiful harvest or other good fortune, perhaps the birth of a child. This rite is conducted in the courtyard by a Brahman priest who reads scriptures. The Limbu claim this ceremony is expensive, and not every household is able or willing to perform it once a year. Sometimes daughters of the household spend days beforehand preparing special foods and making flower leis to decorate the courtyard.

The Limbu household is the center of observances for curing, healing, and the diagnosis of disease by Limbu shamans. Other occasions which call for formalities to safeguard household members are pregnancy, childbirth, and the first rice-eating ceremony for a six-month-old baby.

When a new house is built, the god Okwanāma, supporter of the earth, must be contacted. The blood of a sacrificial pig, plus a few Nepali coins, is placed at the bottom of the center post of the house, connecting symbolically the house and its inhabitants to the center of the world. The workers are fed rice and pork and at night a shaman is invited to conduct a special ritual to Him Sammang, god of the household, at the base of the center post. Since the Limbu do not worship in temples as Hindus do, the house represents not only the abode of earthly existence but the dwelling place of gods and goddesses in the Limbu pantheon.


## Marriage Contracts

Since marriage decisions primarily concern the nuclear families of the bridegroom and the bride, the household plays an important part in marriage arrangements. The bulk of the brideprice, costs of the marriage ceremony, and subsequent payments and gift exchanges must be subtracted from the household budget of the bridegroom. Although the choice of a bride is the exclusive domain of the groom, his father, mother, brothers, and sisters influence his decision because the bride must adjust to her husband's family. If she has a reputation for laziness or frivolity, his family may express dislike. The girl's nuclear family members also are anxious to see her marry a boy whose relatives will treat her well.

Once a commitment has been made, the household has a bearing on the stability of the marriage. The bride, who lives spasmodically in her husband's household for the first two or three years, finds sympathy in her natal home when she quarrels with her in-laws. Her work load is lighter there and the tension of living with strangers is absent. If her family does not feel that she is receiving proper treatment in her husband's household, they may encourage her not to move there right away, which increases the possibilities of her running away with another man. The household of the groom counteracts these negative tendencies by annual gifts sent to the bride's household as well as by the initial brideprice.

The marriage vows must be backed up with the exchange of material goods, hard work, fidelity, and the birth of children, demonstrations that a marriage constitutes more than a temporary love affair. Perhaps similar acts are inherent in the marriage contract in other societies, but the Limbu have institutionalized them into meaningful customs.

Gift exchange at marriage and following the ceremony involves the independent households of the bride and groom, and may even include the members of lineage and pollution groups. The initial costs of a marriage—brideprice and the ceremony itself—are borne almost entirely by the husband's nuclear family.

The two households begin presenting gifts when a man meets his new in-laws and end when the wife dies. If the husband dies, his sons may continue to offer gifts to the wife's natal (their mother's brother's) household as long as she resides in her husband's home. These presentations usually are small amounts of meat and liquor, given on each visit to the wife's homestead, or, in the case of a man's descendants, to their mother's brother's homestead. Gifts will also be presented to other members of the woman's lineage if the household can afford the expense.

We have seen Limbu take alternate routes to avoid meeting the members of their wives' or mother's brother's household because they had no gifts. Gift exchanges symbolize the continuity of a marriage alliance between families because the obligations of a sister's son to his mother's brother are similar to the obligations between a man and his brother-in-law.

The first gifts in a marriage by arrangement are meat, liquor, and beer, which are presented to the bride's parents by an intermediator at the opening of negotiations. In addition, a fee of one rupee is given to the bride's father. Together, these transactions signal the intention of the bridegroom to ask for the girl in marriage.

Acceptance of the gifts obligates the girl's parents to listen to the intermediary's remarks on behalf of the boy and his parents. While the intermediary makes his opening speech, the girl's mother prepares beer and perhaps a meal for the bride-seekers. This thoughtful hospitality is also a token of good faith by the bride and her parents—an indication of seriousness about the negotiations and willingness to part with their daughter if an agreement is reached.

The most important gift is the brideprice, which varies from a token gift to as much as 300 Nepali rupees or their equivalent in livestock, Indian cloth, blankets, gold, silver, or jewelry. The brideprice amount is the subject of the initial negotiations and may require a bit of haggling. The amount of brideprice depends to a great extent on the economic status of the households involved and the circumstances under which the marriage is contracted.

A widow usually receives lesser amounts on her second marriage than on her first, and if she marries her dead husband's brother no brideprice is required. Women who divorce repeatedly command little or no brideprice (see chapter 5) and, although taking another man's wife does not require brideprice, it does involve compensation. A marriage by "theft" or elopement requires the man to pay a brideprice and also a small fine.

Many parents keep the brideprice payment themselves, but sometimes part is given to the bride as jewelry or clothing, to be retained as her personal property, and not necessarily shared with her husband and his family. In her later years she may pass on this property to her daughter, or it may be inherited by her sons when she dies, as part of the family estate. In times of need, it may be sold to help support the family, or used to pay a shaman for his diagnosis and curing rituals.

Our cook had sold all her jewelry to help pay for illnesses of her husband and seven-year-old son. This jewelry had been acquired from her relatives, who received over 100 rupees in brideprice when she married. Because her parents were no longer living at the time of her marriage, she lived in the household of her father's brother, who gave the entire brideprice to her when she went to live with her husband.

If the parents keep the brideprice, they may put it toward acquiring a bride for a marriageable son. In this way brideprice circulates among families. It is seldom used to increase the family fortune through the purchase of land or other tangible property.

Marriages arranged without brideprice seem to be related to the size, composition and relative wealth of the negotiating families. One family living near us had three young unmarried girls and one teenage boy. The family were poor by Limbu standards, and the father said he would not ask for a brideprice for his daughters. Another neighboring family had no sons and two daughters. One girl had already married without brideprice, and the father told us his younger daughter would do the same since he would not have to pay for a son's wedding or marriage payments. Limbu will sometimes forego a brideprice if they feel that a daughter's marriage into a wealthy family might provide greater benefits than money.

Brideprice should be paid to the bride's parents in one installment. Delayed or installment payments are generally frowned upon and when agreed upon usually involve two families which have previously contracted successful marriages together, or two families of high status, which would increase the assurance of brideprice delivery.

The purpose of brideprice payment is twofold: it serves as redress to the girl's parents for the loss of their loved one and her services, and as compensation to the girl's parents to legitimize her future children. In this sense, it is "progeny price" rather than "brideprice."

The acceptance of brideprice ensures delivery of the bride on the wedding day. The parents must make the girl go through with the wedding ceremony, an unpleasant duty for every Limbu girl whose marriage is arranged. No matter how much she approves of her new husband, moving away from her childhood friends and relatives is traumatic. Will her mother-in-law be kind to her? Will she find new friends in a homestead of strangers? Will she have to do work that she has avoided at home? Will her husband buy her clothes and jewelry, or will he use the money for drink or gambling?

The girl's parents are instrumental in helping her to overcome these fears, offering assurances that her husband and in-laws will be kind. They frequently can point out that she has friends and relatives already living there, and a husband who has delivered a generous brideprice will be able to buy her nice things. Few Limbu girls are able to override the pressures from parents and other relatives and avoid the wedding ritual and feast once the brideprice payment has been agreed upon and accepted.

Although payment of the brideprice does insure delivery of the bride to the wedding at the appointed time, it does not insure that she will stay with her husband after the ceremony. If the girl fails to appear at the wedding, which seldom happens, brideprice should be returned in full.

After the wedding ceremony, brideprice is never returned even though partial compensation may be sought. If the bride divorces the groom while still living in her natal home after the wedding, her parents are obligated to pay compensation. If she runs away with another man while living with her parents, they must collect compensation from the new husband (see chapters 5 and 6).

Most Limbu girls return to their natal homes two or three weeks after, if not immediately following, the wedding ceremony. This return signals the start of a rather sensitive time, for now the girl is more likely to resist parental pressures to live permanently with her husband. Only a few days have elapsed between betrothal and the wedding ceremony, and the girl has had little opportunity in that period to make plans with someone else. Her parents, having received the brideprice, have watched her closely. Now, after the wedding, the parents cannot observe her as carefully.

The girl soon settles back into her family routine as if the marriage had been a temporary interruption, and may resume previous courtships with young Limbu men. She may plan divorce if her fears about her new husband and his family were substantiated in the short period she spent with them during and after the wedding. We knew Limbu girls who remained in their natal home for more than five or six years after a wedding ceremony.

Immediately after the wedding ceremony, the groom and his family are obligated to send gifts of money, a whole pig, and liquor to the bride's mother, father, and members of her lineage. A fee of one rupee is given by the groom's agents to the father of the bride on arrival at his home, followed by one rupee as a token of respect, and then a small fee to both parents on entry into their home. The bride's paternal grandparents are presented with gifts of meat and liquor, and all the bride's lineage members receive small amounts of money and liquor. A fee of two rupees is presented to the chief of the bride's lineage, and the bride's mother's brother is presented one or two rupees.

Although we attended five weddings during the course of our field work, we were never able to witness the presentation of these gifts or to discover the actual amount of payments. Caplan (1970:87) records one presentation of 185 rupees, or $18.50, which included porter fees plus fifteen separate gifts of cash, meat, and liquor to the bride's relatives. The value of the gifts depends upon the kinship connections of the bride and the status of her household, but gifts could total 300 or 400 rupees ($30. or $40.) in wealthy families.

The after-ceremony gift is transported by male members of the husband's lineage. A spokesman, probably the intermediator in the marriage negotiations, makes the presentation on behalf of the bridegroom and his household. Transportation expenses are the responsibility of the husband's domestic unit. Although families in the bride's lineage share the gifts, families of the husband's lineage do not usually share in payment. However, if the husband is from a family whose father's siblings have a common *kipat* holding, he will receive financial aid from his father's brothers or secure temporary loans from members of his lineage.

With the acceptance of these gifts, the bride's family is further obligated to see that their daughter stays faithful to her new husband. If the girl lives in her husband's household for a few weeks after the wedding, an additional gift of meat and liquor is sent to the bride's parents when she returns to visit or live with her parents.

Other gifts, called "blessings of meat," are presented annually for three years after the wedding ceremony during the Nepali festival of Dasein in October and November. The first year after the wedding, a gift of two pigs and liquor is brought to the wife's parents by the husband and his relatives. The second year, the payment is one pig and half the original amount of liquor. The third and final payment is half a pig and half the original amount of liquor. The "blessing of meat" does not include cash payments to members of the bride's family.

Brideprice may be forgone in many circumstances, but these gifts are considered obligatory, even in cases of "marriage by theft," elopement or adultery. In "adulterous marriages," the first payment is considerably lower than for arranged marriages, and one presentation of the meat blessing is sufficient. The Limbu will go into debt to make these payments since they strengthen the bond between husband and wife and reaffirm the alliance between their families. Few marriages are dissolved after the final meat blessing has been offered (see chapter 5).

Preparations for the meat blessing payments are made weeks in advance of the Dasein festival. If a family does not own pigs, they are purchased a year ahead and fed until the proper time. A few weeks before payment, liquor is distilled and the bottles are set aside for the occasion. Through kinship connections, the bride's parents are notified when the gifts will be brought to their home. On the appointed day, the pigs are slaughtered and loaded into large carrying baskets. When they arrive, the meat and liquor are displayed in the courtyard or on the front porch of the bride's natal home.

A spokesman asks the bride's parents to accept these gifts as they have the brideprice and to give the couple their blessing for a happy marriage. The father-in-law then wishes his daughter and son-in-law a long life, free from misfortune and filled with children. A meal is prepared and the liquor is served to all the guests who have come to see the gifts. Dasein is a happy festival of visiting and feasting.

The final gift exchange signals the completion of a Limbu marriage. The woman at this time relinquishes her natal patrilineal clan name and assumes that of her husband's clan, as a symbol that she legally belongs to his kin group. This exchange also resolves a problem connected with mourning rites at her death. If a married woman dies prior to the payment of the final gifts, known as the *saimundri* gifts, her husband's clan name is automatically assumed and she attains kinship "by the bone." Kinship "by the bone" in Limbu society means, among other things, that those related under a common clan name are polluted by the death of other clansmen; that is, they are placed in a state of "social death" or ostracism, a liminal state. To relieve this state of pollution a mourning ritual is necessary. In the case of a married woman, the preparations for the mourning ritual cannot begin until after the *saimundri* gifts have been paid. After the payment, the husband's family observes the food taboos associated with the death of a member and accepts the expense of the mourning rituals. If the woman is widowed before the payment is made, her son will assume the responsibility for the mourning rites for his father.

The Limbu describe the final payment as simple: "one bottle of liquor and five pice" (pice are Nepali cents) given to the bride's family by her husband. However, a reciprocal payment from her family is expected to follow, like a dowry. The wife's parents or other members of her natal patrilineage should at this time present the couple with household items—pots, pans, water jugs, rugs or mats, uncooked rice, fermented grain for beer, and other foodstuffs. This blesses the couple for having maintained a long and happy marriage and repays their son-in-law for his acts of kindness and good will expressed in the brideprice and gift exchange.

The final payment and the expected dowry that follows are often delayed for ten to fifteen years after the initial wedding ceremony. Among poorer Limbus, the dowry is ignored altogether and final payment is seldom made until the wife dies. We surveyed thirty women who had been married for more than ten years and only five could claim the completion of the final payment.

*Saimundri* completes the round of gift exchanges in Limbu marriage that begins with the brideprice. It is the final signature to a contractual alliance between Limbu families exchanging women for material goods and services. Limbu marriage thus should be understood as a process rather than an act, since the gift exchanges are extended over several years.

## Inter-ethnic Marriage

Inasmuch as the marriage ceremony and payments differ between the Limbu and high-caste Hindus, intermarriage with the Brahman and Chetri is not thought of as "legitimate" by either group. We knew of only two Limbu and high-caste Hindu "unions," and both were with Brahmans. The high-caste Hindu think that marriage outside their caste is polluting since Brahmans or Chetris will neither accept cooked rice or water from the Limbu nor allow alcoholic beverages at home. Limbu object to inter-ethnic marriages because of cultural differences in language, worship, standard of living, and origin. Marriages or sexual relations between Limbu and the untouchable Hindu castes—blacksmiths, goldsmiths, tailors, and leatherworkers—are forbidden and considered polluting and culturally impossible.

Marriages with Tibetan-speakers and Tamangs are also considered polluting and incompatible because these two groups eat beef, but the restrictions are not nearly as rigid as with the untouchable Hindu castes. The Limbu are aware that in the past they too ate beef, and many consider the rules regarding dietary restrictions to be alien innovations.

Although we knew of no marriages between the Limbu and these two groups, one seventeen-year-old Limbu girl expressed her intention to marry a Tamang boy with whom she had been "courting." The couple's parents refused, and at the time of our field work, the boy and girl were still living in their natal homes.

Marriages between the Limbu and the middle-range Tibeto-Burman speaking castes of Nepal—the Gurung, Magar, and Newar—are permitted by the Limbu, but discouraged by the others. When such a union takes place, the marriage payments and ceremony are concluded in one day and the families of the couple do not visit or exchange gifts. The bridewealth and marriage payments that are intended to strengthen Limbu unions are viewed as irrelevant in cross-cultural marriages.

Marriages to the Rai, especially the neighboring Yakha Rai, are the most common of all intercaste unions in Limbuan (9 percent of recorded marriages) and are legitimate and enduring alliances. The Rai are "brothers" to the Limbu, speak closely related languages and practice similar eating habits, religious beliefs, marriage practices, and bridewealth payments.

Thus, although the Limbu practice tribal endogamy with high- and low-caste Hindus, marriage with non-Limbu is not uncommon with groups such as the Rai. Intercaste marriage is related to social and cultural distance and the societally approved exchange of gifts and bridewealth.


## Gift Exchange in Diverse Types of Marriage

In addition to the arranged marriage *(māgi bihā)*, Limbus recognize two other types: *chori bihā*, or "theft marriage," and *jāri bihā*, or "adulterous marriage." There are a variety of second marriages including the junior levirate, whereby a widow marries the younger brother of her dead husband, and the junior sororate, whereby a widower marries the younger sister of his dead wife. Polygyny is also practiced.

Thefts of unmarried girls *(chori bihā)* and other men's wives *(jāri bihā)* are common and acceptable forms of marriage. The term theft does not imply that a woman has been stolen against her will; it means rather that she has been taken without preliminary negotiations with, and knowledge or approval of, her parents or guardian. Neither "theft marriage" nor "adulterous marriage" is viewed as illegitimate, but a woman who has repeatedly been taken in *jāri* marriage may get a bad reputation as untrustworthy and rather "loose." Theft of an unmarried girl constitutes about 20 percent of all first marriages and wife theft another 20 percent, while about 60 percent of all first marriages are arranged.

"Theft" is one way the Limbu man can avoid the high cost of a formal wedding ceremony. It is akin to elopement and frequently follows a lengthy courtship. Sometimes a couple decides to forgo negotiations because the girl's parents are likely to object to the marriage; sometimes the boy is simply unable to meet the initial brideprice. Eventually, however, he is expected to approach the girl's parents through a mediator with a gift of meat and liquor and a fine of ten to twenty rupees. Future payment is promised, but as one Limbu expressed it, "If the boy cannot pay, what can be done? The marriage has already taken place." A token payment is often sufficient since the girl's parents have little or no control over marriages by "theft."

Marriage by "theft" of another man's wife is somewhat different from "theft" of an unmarried girl. In this case it is "adulterous marriage," and it requires neither a brideprice nor meat blessing payments during the festival of Dasein. Most husbands who take wives in this fashion try to visit the woman's natal home at least once with offerings of meat, liquor, and money, even if the payments constitute only a token. The visits help establish a close affinal link between the families of husband and wife. The final payment is made as in other marriages, since otherwise the woman would be without mourners at her death.

An "adulterous marriage" does however require some immediate compensation to the former husband rather than to the natal kinsmen of the bride. The amount is determined in transactions between new and former husbands and is invariably settled by intermediators, preferably elder men who have kinship connections to both parties. The sum varies with the skill of the negotiators, but the average amount paid in "adulterous marriages" is less than half that of regular marriages. The forsaken husband usually tries to enlist as his spokesman an older male, preferably of his own family or clan, who is familiar with Limbu customs and has the prestige and skills that come with age. Negotiators tend to be of above-average wealth, have considerable influence outside their area of residence, and enjoy reputations as fair men, patient and dignified in conversation. Most are chiefs, since their traditional titles carry prestige.

In polygynous marriages, the husband is expected to pay a brideprice for the second wife as well as the first, especially if she is a virgin. He usually manages to avoid a large ceremony, however, and the costs of taking a second wife are thus reduced. If he "steals" her from her parents he must pay them a fine, as well as brideprice and the subsequent marriage payments. Limbus say that a younger sister of the first wife makes a good second wife because the bridewealth for her will not be as high as for the first and the likelihood of the wives living harmoniously is greatly increased.

Widow remarriage may or may not require a brideprice. Any brideprice paid will be less than that exacted for a virgin bride and will depend upon the bride's age, the length of her previous marriage, and whether or not she actually lived in her deceased husband's household. (One Limbu insisted that a girl would be considered a virgin if she had not lived with her husband and had borne him no children.) Widow remarriage does not always require an elaborate marriage ceremony, particularly if the man and woman are middle-aged and have children. If the couple are in their early twenties or younger, and if neither has had children, the negotiations and the ceremony are similar to an arranged marriage. Such marriages account for only a low percentage of recorded marriages.

Inheritance of an older brother's wife upon his death, called the junior levirate, is acceptable but constitutes less than 2 percent of recorded marriages. In this case brideprice is not obligatory nor is there a big marriage ceremony, but all post-nuptial obligations *(saimundri, etc.)*

should be honored. The Limbu regard brideprice as a progenyprice as well, since it is a payment made for the childbearing potential of the bride as well as for her sexual favors. It is for this reason that a levirate brideprice is considered unnecessary: the payments have already been fulfilled by the deceased older brother. In a sororate marriage where a man inherits a dead wife's younger sister, brideprice is paid as with any other arranged marriage. If the sister is a virgin bride the price will be higher than if she has been married, but it will still be less than that expected for the first wife. Both levirate and sororate marriages are contracted with natal, not classificatory, brothers and sisters.

The low number of marriages involving the levirate or sororate is difficult to understand, since many Limbu readily claim it is a "good thing." Age differences between the couples and the freedom that the Limbu girls and boys have in choosing their spouses are probable factors. In at least one recorded case, a sororate marriage ended when the dead wife's sister, almost twenty years younger than her husband, ran off with another man.

A joking relationship between males and females who are potential marriage partners in the junior levirate and sororate is common. This flirtatious situation occasionally leads to sexual relations before the death of the brother's wife or the sister's husband and is grounds for divorce. We knew of two such instances that were the subject of lively gossip. In one, the husband divorced his wife, who had been sleeping with his younger brother, by sending her home. He then forced his brother not only to leave his house but to get out of Limbuan permanently. The second case, an adulterous relationship between a man's wife and his younger brother, did not result in divorce, but the husband and his wife moved to Assam, returning from time to time.

Although the junior levirate and sororate are acceptable to, and even encouraged by, many Limbu, marriages or sexual relations between a woman and her husband's *elder* brother or between a man and his wife's *elder* sister are "sinful." Social intercourse between these relatives is usually strained and characterized on both sides by an attitude of respect and extreme politeness. They do not completely avoid each other, but when in the presence of his wife's elder sister, a Limbu man does not look directly into his sister-in-law's eyes. Direct conversation is subdued, and if speaking Nepali the two will use the high-grade honorific pronoun and verb forms. Caplan (1966:245) records two cases of men who married their dead wives' older sisters, but it was "considered to be an unsavory practice" and required a special payment of a fine to the wife's family.

## Sex Roles in Kinship and Marriage

Many Limbu social and kinship customs place women in a subordinate position to men. Descent lines and inheritance partially exclude women. After marriage, the woman is expected to reside in the home of her husband and in the village of his patrilineage. Her importance in home maintenance and the continuity of property and titles is acknowledged through bridewealth and gift exchange, to be sure, but these institutions, too, keep her in a position of servitude and subordination to male authority.

We have seen how men negotiate for women in arranged marriages and pay a brideprice for them. In "bride theft," men are presumed to be the aggressors, even though the women they elope with more often than not go of their own free will. The "theft" of another man's wife also expresses male dominance in the way the men involved negotiate about compensation and bridewealth payments. Polygyny is a double standard not offset by polyandry; that is, a man may have more than one wife at a time but a woman must remain faithful to one man.

In sum, Limbu women appear to be merely objects used by men as weak sisters, sexual satisfiers, labor resources, and childbearers. In this perspective, Limbu women come across as little more than spectators at male-dominated power games. It is a stereotypical view of Limbu society but as this chapter reveals, it has some basis in fact.

The Limbu themselves define their social life by sexual prejudice. For example, when genealogies are traced, women are "forgotten" after two or three generations. Homes and homesteads are identified with male heads rather than women and boys are prized over girls. Women do not hold political office nor can they expect to openly question male decisions without repercussions. At meals, men are served first while women wait until the youngest male in the household has eaten. When a family walks together the men go first, unencumbered by burdens and conversing freely with passers-by, while the women trail behind, lugging food, cooking utensils, and babies. When visitors come to the home, women often fade into the background to cook meals and care for children.

The unattached woman perhaps fares somewhat better. Although descent and inheritance are centered around males, unmarried women can inherit land and properties. A sister's portion of the inheritance is somewhat less than her brothers', but she does not have a family to care for since she is not married. Unmarried women share equally with men in the decision-making process about planting, harvesting, and the mortgage and sale of land.

A widow is allowed to remain on her deceased husband's land, occupy his household, and retain a portion of his inheritance, as long as she does not remarry. What is more, widows often become powerful figures in their own right in Limbuan. A number of our neighbors were widows who lived with their daughters. These women were never ignored in the day-to-day decision-making process, and were consulted in disputes over bridewealth, *jāri* compensation, and other matters affecting the family. Many times, elderly widows assumed the role of "matriarch" in household clusters, and their authority was paid ritual homage on such important ceremonial and festival occasions as Dasein, the birth of a child, or the first rice-eating ceremony for an infant. During household sacrifices, these widows were sent portions of meat or liquor by close relatives as a token of respect.

But even among the married women the situation is not as one-sided as it might seem. Female-dominated households have increased in this century owing to the long-term absenteeism of men, and this development has fostered new patterns of female authority. Today these patterns are beginning to extend even to households where men reside year-round. With the advent of a cash economy and the need for supplementary income, women contribute substantially to the maintenance of the household through labor and the sale of cloth and liquor. Limbu men have begun to recognize that women have valuable business sense, and to seek out, even defer to, their opinions about the household budget, the purchase and sale of animals, and other business relationships that formerly were exclusive provinces of men. We were surprised at the openness of women in day-to-day decision making in the household and community.

Women control the money they earn. They commonly use it to buy seed grain, livestock, household utensils, clothing for their children, and other items to benefit the entire household. Sometimes, however, they invest it in jewelry and other personal property over which they maintain exclusive control—and indeed Limbu men are increasingly encouraging such independence. While surveying married women in a return visit to Limbuan in the fall of 1975, Rex repeatedly encountered situations in which women claimed personal ownership of livestock that on the surface appeared to be the household property of males. The men readily confirmed these claims and often pointed out that a certain animal was purchased with profits the woman earned from the sale of liquor or cloth. Nearly all of the eighty-six married women interviewed in three Limbu villages owned at least one animal that had been purchased from such profits.

Because of their new-found economic control women are in a strong position to influence a son's marriage by giving him some or all of the brideprice and marriage payments. They may also sway the decision of their daughters' marriages and overrule their husband's wishes, even in arranged marriages.

Many young girls are allowed to keep part or all of the brideprice as a personal dowry in arranged marriages. Thus they enter their new husband's household with some economic independence: a woman who retains her bridewealth must be regarded by her husband and his household on more equal terms, as an asset beyond her labor and childbearing potential.

Thus a number of avenues are open to Limbu women, economically, politically, and socially—and all point to the independence of females within male-dominated social institutions. Women are able to modify these institutions in ways that may not conform strictly to the rules of Limbu society. In the remaining chapters, we will examine how these processes affect the stability of marriage.

# Getting Married

## 4

Premarital courtship through dancing allows freedom of choice in marriage for young partners, even in cases of arranged marriage. Limbu boys and girls are thus able to meet a variety of potential mates and make their favorites known to their parents, who then presumably attempt to arrange marriages accordingly. In courtship, the sexes meet on equal grounds, symbolically and in reality. The dance also affords Limbu young people an opportunity to elope or run away with their preferred mates if their parents choose to ignore their desires.

The nature and importance of a Limbu woman's role in marriage are symbolized in a number of ways during the betrothal proceedings and the wedding ceremony. The bridegroom and his family humble themselves figuratively in front of the bride and her family in proposals of marriage, and receive "insults" and "abuse" from the bride's father. During the two-day wedding ceremony in the bridegroom's home, members of the bridal party are treated with deference and exaggerated respect and housed and served in a separate dwelling constructed especially for them. The ceremony itself is punctuated with symbolic acts of defiance by the bride, counteracted with symbolic acts which demonstrate her subservience. She kneels at the feet of her new husband in respect, and she ritually sweeps the home, cleans the courtyard, and carries water. The wedding ceremony is like a dramatic performance in which the roles of men and women conflict and are then resolved.

## Courtship and the Rice Dance

The rice dance, an integral part of courtship which plays a role in all Limbu marriages, is unique to the more conservative castes and ethnic groups of Nepal because of the freedom it occasions among young people in the choice of marriage partners. This flexibility represents a historical adaptation to shifting economic and political conditions in eastern Nepal and reinforces Limbu cultural exclusiveness.

A courtship dance is an informal affair that may be preplanned by the participants or may begin spontaneously. Only two people are required, but more commonly ten to twenty are involved. Large gatherings occur at major festivals such as Dasein or Tihar, which are held in autumn throughout Nepal. Weekly markets, where villagers sell produce and other items, also present opportunities for performing the rice dance, as do carnivals held throughout the dry season in Limbuan. But most of the dancing takes place in the courtyards of private homes. The participants are boys and girls of marriageable age, and the dance itself is the Limbu form of "dating."

According to legend, the dance originally had a supremely practical purpose. Nowadays, the Limbu use oxen to thresh rice as most Nepali do, but in the olden days it had to be threshed by hand, which was a tedious job. Supposedly, an old man named Shorokpa proposed a way to accomplish the work enjoyably. He summoned the young people of his village to a courtyard strewn with rice sheaves and instructed them to stand in a line (first a boy, then a girl) and hold hands. Then, by raising alternate feet in unison, they were to trample the sheaves. As they trampled, the circle of dancers sang songs and moved around the surface of the courtyard. Older people followed their progress and exchanged the threshed rice stalks for fresh ones.

Variations on this story all confirm that the rice dance was originally primarily utilitarian and only later came to be associated with courtship. The changing purpose probably corresponds to the large-scale immigration into Limbuan of the Hindu, who brought their methods of threshing paddy with oxen.

Today, each province in Limbuan has a different style of dance although the rules remain the same. Dancers first move five steps to the right, then five steps to the left, and finally three steps in the same spot. After these thirteen steps, the dancers turn to the right and begin again. The person at the far right of the line starts the dance by singing a chorus, and the other dancers join in. There are no musical instruments, but the rhythms of song and dance complement one another. The songs are invariably love songs and are sung wherever Limbu meet—at carnivals, markets, weddings, and festivals.

Early in the morning on the first day we entered Limbuan, we saw a rice dance. There were only three dancers—two girls and a boy who, according to onlookers, had been dancing all night. To our untutored eyes that morning, the dance appeared to consist of a mere shuffling of feet and a sing-song mumbling of words—not at all the exotic performance we had been led to expect by non-Limbu informants who had described the custom as shockingly provocative. During the course of our field work, we witnessed twenty to thirty rice dances, involving as few as two individuals and as many as thirty. The dance is very important to the Limbu, who take great pains in learning the footwork and the accompanying songs because the dance is an invitation to courtship and marriage.

## Rules of the Rice Dance

There are a number of rigidly enforced rules involved in the dance which express Limbu attitudes toward marriage. The most important is that a boy and a girl of the same clan are not allowed to dance together just as no two members of the same clan are allowed to have sexual relations or to marry.

At one dance we witnessed during a carnival, a young Limbu girl spectator suddenly sprang up and jerked another girl out of the line. We asked her why she had interrupted the dance and she answered disbelievingly, "The girl was of the Tumbahangphe clan and so was the boy. Should persons of the same clan dance together?" The participants were unaware of their error, since it was the first time they had met. In the pattern of courtship, only potentially marriageable partners should dance together.

Non-Limbu Nepalis assert, through innuendo, that the dance is an immediate prelude to sexual relations. It is true that the dances take place at night and are seldom chaperoned by parents, but the ones we attended and the few in which we participated hardly seemed likely settings for clandestine love affairs. Partners are not even allowed to touch toes, much less to make intimate advances. Hand-holding is the only physical contact allowed; any other contact between partners calls for a formal request for pardon on both sides.

The Limbu recognize that the code of the dance is not always strictly observed because secret meetings sometimes ensue, but these exceptions

74

are frowned upon. A number of divorces or broken marriages have resulted from young married girls finding lovers at a dance and subsequently leaving their husbands. But for the most part, the dance is an avenue for the selection of future spouses rather than an institutionalized means for deception and sexual promiscuity.

The non-Limbu misunderstanding of the dance sometimes tragically widens the cultural gap between the Limbu and immigrants. One case of a Brahman man who joined a dance at the weekly market in Panchthar province was told us by a Peace Corps volunteer who had lived there. Apparently the Brahman felt that a fifteen-year-old Limbu girl was making advances to him during the course of the dance, so he dragged her into the woods and raped her. The Limbu of the area, outraged by the act, presented him the options of leaving the bazaar or facing prosecution in the courts.

Husbands and wives should never dance together nor do old people participate, but young married men and women may join the dance when their spouses are away. This usually occurs before a couple has children, and prior to the wife's move from her natal home, seldom after a man and wife have set up their household.

Limbu marriages require a two- to three-year trial period after the initial ceremony. A young bride, after spending a short time in her new husband's home, will usually return to her natal home until after the birth of her first child. During this period, relations between the husband and wife are tense, and either one or both may continue courtship with other young people until the marriage is on a firmer footing. If a dance should take place near the natal home of the girl and her husband does not attend, she might dance the entire night with a new partner. A husband whose wife is not living with him might instigate a dance to meet new girls or to relieve the boredom of a humdrum existence.

In a homestead near us in Limbuan, three newly married teenage girls lived with their natal kinsmen and participated in dances during most weekly markets. The youngest was visited by a male friend, reason enough for a dance, particularly if he brought other young boys to dance with her natal kinswomen. This rice dance "partnership" led to tensions in the marriage. When her husband, who lived about a day's walk away, learned of her activities, they quarreled and he took a second wife. Then the girl's dancing became more fervent and defiant and she justified her activities by blaming her husband. He finally visited the homestead and demanded that his wife return to live with him. She refused, saying, "He has a wife now. Why should I live with him?" With the help of her father and on the basis of a recent Nepali marriage law, she sought a legal divorce from her husband because he took a second wife. When we left Limbuan the dispute had not been settled, but the girl still lived in her natal home and continued to participate in the dance. Seven years later, when Rex again visited Limbuan, she had obtained a divorce, was married to a Limbu in the Nepali police force, and was nursing a two-year-old baby boy. She recalled her stormy first marriage with laughter and proclaimed her happiness with her new husband.

Meanwhile, although this young woman's two married kinswomen also participated frequently in dances, tensions never surfaced in their marriages in the time we remained in Limbuan. Before we left, the older girl gave birth to a boy and her husband eventually moved her and the child to his home in a remote province. She was reluctant to leave her natal home, but the marriage was essentially sound and divorce or separation appeared extremely unlikely. The second girl had not conceived a child but her marriage appeared stable and her husband, wealthy by Limbu standards, showered her and her mother with gifts. This girl, however, was reluctant to move to his village because her mother was widowed and old and would be alone. Seven years later both of these women were again interviewed. The first, as predicted, was very happy with her now seven-year-old son. The second had exceeded all expectations. Not only had she divorced and managed to keep much of the wealth of her former marriage; she had remarried and even persuaded her second husband to allow her to stay with her widowed mother. Her independence was highly visible in relation to the other young women in the area, as she was by far the wealthiest of all the women interviewed in the three villages.

Courtship through the dance sometimes continues even after the birth of children. For example, when our thirty-year-old cook/translator, mother of two, accompanied us to act as guide and assistant at distant weddings, she would participate in the dance. Her Limbu friends did not approve of her behavior but said little because when a husband is away for a long time, as hers was, such behavior is not surprising. She was the object of gossip nonetheless, and no doubt a few married women secretly applauded her courage.

The rules of the dance are more lenient for husbands than for wives. No one thinks twice about the participation of a young married man whose wife is childless and still resides in her natal home. One young Limbu man we knew danced even though his wife was residing in his home. In this case, however, there were no children and the wife had formerly been married to someone else. Their alliance was an "adulterous marriage" which had directly resulted from a dance. His kinsmen speculated that he would soon take a second wife to bear children, and the dance provided him with good opportunities to seek out available females. On a number of occasions he arranged dances near his homestead and several times borrowed our radio to impress young girls with it at a dance.

In cases of "wife theft," divorce, and adultery, the Limbu commonly cite the dance as the reason for the failure of the marriage: "They danced together and fell in love, so the woman left her husband," or, "After dancing, they fell in love and had a child, so what can you do?" Limbu of course understand that the causes of divorce run deeper than that, but they also recognize that when a husband or wife starts dancing with new partners it is a sign of a shaky marriage. Marital tensions, jealousies, fears, and other dissatisfactions almost always eventually culminate in dancing.

## Courtship Dance Partners

When unmarried boys and girls who have reached puberty take rice dance partners in Limbuan, it signifies much the same relationship as "going steady" in the United States. Dance partnership is not the same as engagement, and it entails no formal rights, obligations, or duties. It does mean that the boy and girl admit to a kind of "love" relationship or infatuation—and this commitment gives rise to endless gossip by the peer group, especially the girls.

We do not know how many dancing partners are likely to marry each other, but clearly marriage does not necessarily follow spontaneous attachment. We witnessed numerous instances where dancing partnerships were dissolved because the males simply stopped visiting the girls' homesteads. Obviously these relationships were merely temporary infatuations. An average individual will probably have many dancing partners between the times of puberty and marriage; indeed, a young male who moves around a lot may have a number of dancing partners simultaneously, after the manner of the sailor with a girl in every port. His many "dancing friends" are likely to live in widely scattered villages and never know to what extent they must compete for his attention.

## The Rice Dance at Weddings

The most important occasion for a dance is the Limbu wedding ceremony, which involves two or three days of feasting and celebrating. The unmarried boys and girls get together and dance all night. Future marriages are likely because most of the eligible males are from the bridegroom's village and clan while the girls are from the bride's village and clan. Since in the ideal Limbuan marriage pattern brothers of one clan marry sisters of another, the wedding dance offers an opportunity for young people sharing this preferred relationship to meet. Any marriages that result from such meetings have a good prospect of success. The normal tensions between in-marrying females and those already residing in the husband's homestead are greatly eased when the women share common backgrounds of kinship and residence. Even if no promising liaisons result, the relaxed and festive atmosphere of the wedding dance helps to cement existing in-law relationships and smooth the way for the newly married couple.

Apart from the special relationship between the dancers, the rice dance performed at weddings differs from dances on other occasions in that the likelihood of more intimate get-togethers is reduced because older relatives are present. The bride's parents never attend their daughter's wedding ceremony, but the bride, her unmarried sisters, and her young cousins are accompanied by her clan brothers and paternal uncles and aunts, who act as chaperones.

## The Uniqueness of Limbu Courtship Patterns

The courtship dance is apparently purely a Limbu custom and contrasts sharply with the customs of other Nepali castes and ethnic groups. Among the more Hinduized Nepalis of the eastern hills, especially the Brahman and Chetri who have immigrated to Limbuan, courtship seldom precedes marriage. Hindu marriages are usually arranged by the parents, and the young men and women have little to do with selection of a spouse or the nuptial negotiations. The very idea that a society would condone a man's dancing publicly with a prospective mate is considered shocking among the non-Limbu. The Limbu, on the other hand, while recognizing that it may sometimes lead to such abuses as "wife theft" and extramarital relations, regard it as an entirely legitimate avenue toward the formation of stable marriages.

Limbu women in particular gain greater than usual freedom benefits from the dance. It is true that it is the Limbu male and his kinship group who ultimately make the mate selection and launch the negotiations of the marriage contract. But in the meantime the dance allows a woman to look over the field of available males, and to pass judgment on them and make her judgments known to those who will contract her marriage. And if her free choice in arranged marriages is circumscribed by the betrothal proceedings, she still can exercise her right of refusal from the perspective gained in courtship experience.

Again thanks to the dance, many Limbu marriages can be characterized as "love marriages." The romantic love that is an integral part of the rice dance is most readily reflected in the songs the dance inspires. Limbu boys and girls also sing these songs while working in the fields or walking on the trails—songs that celebrate the beauty of a girl and of the night, that compare the dance and the dancers to trees, flowers, stars, and the moon. The following is an example of a courtship song recorded and freely translated by Chemjong (1967:94–95):

> We two and all are friends,
> Let us pick up the flowers of Sekmari and go to dance paddy.
> As we have seen young fish moving and dancing,
> So we shall dance together.
> The dancers have gathered
> And spread in a circle, like the Setlo song flowers,
> We came happily to dance
> And will disperse happily after dance.

Even old people who no longer dance remember courtship songs and sing them to pass the time or to recall the happiness and fond memories of their youth. Thus the dance provides not only the manifest and obvious function of an avenue to marriage but has a latent or secondary function as a source of entertainment to relieve the boredom that arises out of the drudgery of hill life.

A rarer form of courtship takes place through singing contests. If a boy and girl become infatuated, the boy may take the initiative and compose spontaneous love songs. The girl is expected to reply, and the result is a musical exchange that goes on until one partner begs off. If the boy wins this "song duel," the girl is expected to marry him, and the usual procedures of a Limbu marriage follow—bridewealth and gifts to the girl's parents. If the girl wins, the relationship is ended, presumably because a boy could never control a wife whom he cannot even defeat in a song match.

We witnessed only one song duel, delivered in jest by a long-married middle-aged man to an old woman. The two were slightly tipsy and began singing while walking along the trail leading to the weekly market, much to the amusement of passers-by. Song duels ordinarily take place in private when a couple is in the fields or in the jungles gathering fodder for animals, and are seldom observed.

## The Rites of Betrothal

A new marriage is fraught with underlying anxieties and frustrations and the critical relations between husband, wife, and in-laws are reflected in the betrothal and marriage proceedings. For the husband there is the problem of finances. He and his family must be able to meet the expense of a large wedding, the entertainment of guests, and the initial gifts in marriage. Many times in arranged marriages the husband and wife have met no more than two or three times and hardly know each other. For the wife marriage means an abrupt change in her whole life. She must nerve herself to enter a household of strangers, people who will for many years dominate her every movement. The focus of this change is her new mother-in-law, and it is no wonder that the prime topic of conversation among young, newly married girls is the behavior and personality characteristics of mothers-in-law.

In arranged marriages, once a young man decides to marry, he confers with his father and other patrilineal kinsmen who determine if they can afford the expense of the brideprice and ceremony. Usually the boy has reached the age of eighteen or nineteen, and has demonstrated that he is capable of the duties and obligations of adulthood. He has been able to meet and court a number of girls of marriageable age and learn something about their personalities, their families and the expected brideprice.

The age at which Limbu girls should marry is set at around sixteen, but of the five weddings we attended, two of the brides were hardly more than fourteen. We knew of only one instance in which a girl had reached her twenties without having married, and she had expressed intentions never to marry. The wife's age is usually within two or three years of the husband's if the couple are young and both marrying for the first time.

Most Limbu weddings take place during the months of February and March, the Nepali month of Phagan, which is considered an auspicious month. In Tehrathum during this month we attended five Limbu weddings within a six-mile radius and noted at least six others. Numerous Chetri, Brahman, Newar, and menial caste weddings occur at this time also. The most inauspicious month is Saun (mid-July to mid-August), when the pantheon of Limbu and Hindu deities go underground "to cook rice and prepare food." All rituals except funerals are postponed during this month.

## The Role of the Intermediator

The first marriage is arranged by the prospective bridegroom through an intermediator and patterns of avoidance between in-laws are symbolized through his role. The intermediator should be a member of the bride-groom's patrilineal kin group, older than the bridegroom and closely related genealogically, but *never* the bridegroom's father.

Behind this last proviso lies the most extreme example of Limbu avoidance between in-laws: the young bridegroom's parents should not meet the young bride's parents. That is why the bride's parents attend the wedding of their daughter only in unusual circumstances, such as an elopement, and never appear at an arranged marriage. Even after the couple have produced children, their parents seldom meet under the same roof, and if they do conversation and social intercourse is strained and exaggeratedly polite. Before the birth of a child they avoid association entirely.

It is preferable for the intermediator to be a patrilineal relative who has already established relations through marriage with the girl's family. A father's brother who is married to a woman from the bride's patrilineage would be an excellent choice, since he would know the bride's kinsmen and have some ties with her parents. The ideal candidate would be an elder brother or classificatory elder brother of the bridegroom who has married a sister or classificatory sister of the prospective bride. Here the intermediator would have the same in-law relationship to the bride's parents as the bridegroom and negotiations would fall into a pattern set by precedent, thus reducing uncertainties and tensions between bride-groom and parents-in-law. Furthermore, since the bride would be marrying into a family in which one or more women from her natal group were already living, conflicts with her mother-in-law would be minimized and she would embark upon her duties in the new household amid familiar faces.

When he begins his journey with the intermediator to search for a bride, the bridegroom usually has a number of girls in mind as alternative choices should the negotiations with the parents of his first choice prove unsatisfactory. He might also be prepared for stiff resistance. One wedding we witnessed, between a wealthy young Limbu of Tehrathum district and a girl from Taplejung took place only after long negotiations. Although the details were sketchy, we learned that after his first overtures the girl had refused to go with him, and subsequently her parents had balked at the brideprice offer because they knew the boy's father was a wealthy ex-Gurkha soldier with a handsome pension and a large parcel of land.

At the home of the bride's parents, bridegroom, intermediator, and prospective in-laws discuss crops and the weather, or simply gossip for a while. The intermediator talks while the bridegroom sits quietly, nodding his head and attempting to play down his role in the proceedings. After the intermediator and the bridegroom have been treated to food and drink, the intermediator announces the intent of the visit. The girl and her parents usually know the purpose before he speaks, thanks to the highly efficient grapevine that transmits rumor over great distances with startling speed in the hills of Nepal. Moreover, they may well have reached a decision on the matter, unless they have doubts about the size of the brideprice that will be offered. Nevertheless, out of courtesy they remain silent for the moment.

The first visit is a formality except for the negotiations over brideprice. After the intentions of the visit are announced, the bride's parents break their silence to address the bridegroom and the intermediator in gruff, superior tones of voice and demand an inordinately large brideprice. The parents praise the qualities of their daughter, claiming she is a hard worker, an asset to the family and impossible to replace. The suitor may be told to wait as a matter of ritual on the asserted grounds that "it is our custom," particularly if the bride's family has a higher economic status than his own. This initial conversation between the intermediator and the bridegroom's future in-laws is but the first in a chain of symbolic acts intended to demonstrate the superior status of wife-giver to that of wife-receiver.


## The Wedding Ceremony

Once an agreement has been reached, the bridegroom and the intermediator return home. Invitations to the ceremony are sent to relatives, friends, and neighbors, and preparations are made for the marriage feast. Rice and a water buffalo or other meat must be purchased to feed the bridal party and guests. Beer is brewed and liquor is distilled or purchased to be served to high-ranking guests. A family of the tailor caste is requested to sew the garments worn by the bride and bridegroom.

On the appointed day, intermediator and bridegroom journey to the bride's home with the brideprice. After payment, they escort her and the bridal party to the groom's home. Temporary living quarters for the bridal party are constructed a short distance from the bridegroom's house, usually in an unplanted field.

The expenses of the wedding ceremony, mostly assumed by the husband's household, may reach astronomical figures by Limbu standards. We could not accurately tabulate the costs of any of five ceremonies we attended, but none of them were less than five hundred Nepali rupees, or about fifty dollars. In two of these cases the total costs of the rice, beer, and meat alone amounted to more than fifty dollars. Estimated costs for the largest wedding we attended were:

| | |
|---|---|
| Rice | 300.00 Rupees |
| Beer | 150.00 |
| Liquor | 40.00 |
| Meat | 400.00 |
| Cloth for groom's garment | 25.00 |
| Cloth for bride's garment | 40.00 |
| Total estimated costs | 995.00 Rupees ($95.00) |

This expenditure was for the wedding of a high-status couple; other weddings we attended probably cost half as much. If goat meat or chicken or pig is served, expenses mount. All guests were served water buffalo meat at weddings we attended, but honored guests received specially prepared foods, such as chicken, pork, or goat. Sometimes weddings are attended by members of other castes and ethnic groups— the Magar or Gurung, for example—who will not eat pork. Then a goat might be slaughtered especially to feed such guests, with the rest of the meat served to the bridal party. Outlays for the wedding ceremony depend on the number of guests invited and the amount of beer or liquor served. A Limbu family's social status and prestige can be gauged by the money spent at its wedding ceremonies.

Once the bride and her entourage arrive at the groom's home, they are the center of attention. On the first day the bride and her friends and relatives are sheltered near the homestead of the bridegroom. The bridegroom's parents meet the group and see that they are settled comfortably in a temporary shelter constructed of bamboo and thatch. Every effort is made by the bridegroom's relatives to take care of the bridal party's needs and to ensure them a plentiful supply of beer, which is served in bamboo or wooden containers with bamboo straws. The beer is prepared by placing fermented grain in these containers and pouring hot water over it. The grain is filtered out of the beverage by the straws. Limbus ordinarily strain their beer into brass bowls or containers before serving it, but for honored guests the beer containers are brought out. Spicy hors d'oeuvres are served with the beer. Then the groom's father addresses the bridal party: "We welcome you to our village with these humble gifts of food. We are your servants. Is the beer good? Is the food good? Whatever your needs may be, summon us at once. Do not be shy. We are here to serve you."

Next, preparations for a full-course meal begin. The bridegroom's relatives fire guns to signal that the bridal party has arrived and settled in, and the wedding festivities are about to begin. Messengers take personal invitations to relatives and friends. People of nearby homesteads, usually lineage-mates of the bridegroom, come to meet the bride and her party, to drink beer, and to talk, and assist in the preparation of food. Once the bridal party has been served a meal and their beer containers refilled, they retire. If young unmarried males of the bridegroom's village come to meet the bridal party, a rice dance may be organized for the night.

On the morning following the arrival of the bridal party, guests come into the homestead and sit around drinking beer and gossiping. The bridal party is served a breakfast, but not all are on hand to receive it. If the girls and boys in the party have danced the night before they may spend the morning resting. In any event, everyone is tired from the journey, which may have been a two- to three-day walk.

As the day progresses, men appear at the homestead with large double-headed drums and dance in the courtyard. The drum dance is performed only at weddings and, in the Tehrathum district, only by men. During our stay in Limbuan, nothing else matched the intensity and excitement of this dance. Twenty or thirty dancers, each with a drum, move in a circle, kick their feet, swirl and stomp the earth to the coordinated beat of the drums. A leader improvises steps and movements. There is no "club" or "order" for these dancers; every adult male Limbu qualifies, although their skills vary. At weddings, the adults rest between dances while young boys often beat the drums and attempt to learn the steps. When the boys reach puberty, they will dance too.

The dancers usually live in or near the village of the bridegroom, but good dancers from even two or three days' walk away are sent invitations. The drum dance is a purely Limbu art form; no other caste or ethnic group in Nepal uses the same kind of drums or knows the intricate steps that go into the dance. The drums too are Limbu-made, unlike other musical instruments in Nepal which are made by the untouchable Hindu castes. They consist of hollowed-out logs with buffalo or goatskin stretched over them. They are struck by hand or by a short stick with a string of bells attached which produces a tinkling sound that complements the heavy thud of percussion.

The circle dance provides most of the entertainment and background for the activity during the first day of the wedding while food and beer are prepared for a late afternoon communal meal. During the day more guests arrive and either join in the dance or the preparations, or sit around the courtyard talking, gossiping, and laughing.

Tailors spend most of the first day sewing wedding garments, sitting to the side of the main courtyard with sewing machines, needles, and thread. Members of the tailor caste play an important role in the Limbu wedding ceremony, but always as servants. They are also musicians and entertainers, accompanying the wedding procession with drums, flutes, and trumpets, and on the second day of the festivities offering blessings to the bride and bridegroom in the hope of receiving gifts from the guests.

At one wedding we attended, the animals were killed in the morning and the meat for the communal meal was shown to the bridal party for approval. This was but one more gesture intended to symbolize the subordinate status of bride receivers and to indicate an attitude of deference to the bridal party. Such gestures serve to enhance one of the more important secondary functions of the entire wedding celebration: to allay tensions between bride and bridegroom and their relatives.

In the late afternoon the wedding ceremony gets under way. The groom comes into the courtyard, accompanied by his younger unmarried brothers and sisters, wearing the newly tailored wedding garments. A gun is fired to signal the guests and latecomers that the procession to meet the bridal party is about to commence.

The groom is dressed in white, the color for marriage and for funerals. He wears white trousers, a white tunic, and a white cap. Garlands of flowers are placed around his neck and on his cap. His forehead displays a decoration of rice mixed with milk and yogurt which symbolizes his parents' blessing. He may also wear one or more bandoleers (belts over the shoulder) made of silver and gold. The bride wears the clothing presented to her by the bridegroom, a fine brightly colored linen or silk sari from India or Malaya, and a black velvet blouse. A brightly colored shawl hides her blushing and nervousness. She wears a great deal of gold and silver jewelry and, to symbolize her new status, a green beaded necklace with interlaced golden ornaments.

The bridegroom's procession is led to the bridal party by the drum dancers and the tailor musicians. The bridegroom and his attendants and guests follow. A special attendant, a younger brother, walks by the groom's side and holds a large umbrella above his head. Behind these two, the groom's sisters or unmarried female cousins carry brass vases filled with flowers and trays of uncooked rice, flowers, and water. Guns are fired and the bride appears with her party. The drum dancers circle

## The Limbu Wedding

*Above:* A bride (center) sits with members of her bridal party before the wedding ceremony. *Below:* A bridal party drinks beer from bamboo *thongbā*. *Above right:* A reluctant bride is readied for the wedding ceremony by members of the bridal party. *Below right:* Three Limbu men wait to signal the beginning of a wedding procession with shotgun fire.

*Above:* The wedding ceremony starts when the bride and groom meet on the trail, accompanied by their friends and relatives. *Below:* The *chaubrung* drum dancers provide excitement and entertainment throughout the wedding. *Above right:* A Limbu shaman instructs the bride and groom at the final wedding ceremony. *Below right:* Members of the tailor caste play instruments at the wedding.

the bridal party three times, while the bride hides among her friends and relatives, embarrassed and shy.

This marks the first stage of the wedding ceremony, which continues another day. Bridal clothes are presented by the female escorts of the groom, and the bride is expected to don the clothing, surrounded by her party, and step forth to meet her husband with humility and gratitude. Acceptance of the gift is the bride's first public acknowledgement that she is willing to enter into matrimony—hence her embarrassment and show of reluctance. At one wedding, the bride refused altogether to put the clothes on, despite all the pleadings and proddings of the older women in her party. After fifteen or twenty minutes of pleading and balking, she finally yielded grudgingly and was literally dressed by her bridal party.

After the bride is dressed, the couple stand face-to-face and exchange garlands of flowers. A timid bride—or a recalcitrant one—may have to be aided by her relatives in this exchange as well. She must drop to her knees, bow, and touch the feet of her groom with her forehead to signify submission to his authority. When this act has been performed, the guests and relatives shout their approval, musicians play trumpets and flutes, and the drum dancing resumes vigorously.

The joyful procession now moves toward the groom's homestead for the communal meal, the bride borne on the shoulders of her younger brother. At the homestead a straw mat is laid down for the couple, who are coaxed to sit down and be served their first meal together. The bride hides her face in her shawl and resists her friends' admonishments to be proud of her new status. She may turn her back on the bridegroom to avoid sitting too close in public. The bridegroom stares blankly ahead to conceal his bashfulness. The guests and relatives try to ease tensions with forced laughter and joking.

The procession are seated in a line to be served, bride and bridegroom first, followed by bride's relatives, then other guests. The meal is eaten rapidly, Nepali style. When the guests have rinsed their mouths, they filter back to the courtyard for the next stage of the ceremony.

The bridegroom's father and mother stand at the doorway of their home, while other relatives face each other three or four feet apart in lines extending into the courtyard. Guests and spectators crowd behind, and a path from the courtyard to the doorway is created for the wedding march. A wooden plank is laid next to the front porch, flanked by dishes of rice, flowers, and vases of water. The bride walks up the path, along the plank, and into the doorway as onlookers throw rice and sprinkle water at her to symbolize approval of the marriage. She is also given a rice blessing on her forehead by the parents and siblings of the bridegroom. The bridegroom, escorted by his younger brother, also receives his parents' blessing.

The couple enter the house and are seated side-by-side on a straw mat, backs to the wall, facing the center post. A vase of flowers, water, and uncooked rice is placed in front of them and oil lamps are lit. The shaman faces the couple and merrymaking relatives and guests crowd into the room, shouting and laughing. Everyone voices an opinion, and in many ways the proceedings begin to take on the aspect of a drunken brawl.

In the middle of the confusion, which sometimes lasts for more than an hour, the shaman chants sacred Limbu myths and legends about the origin of the rice dance, the drum dance, and marriage customs, and recites details of the Limbu marriage law. He is answered periodically by old men who remember parts of the myths and shout their answers exuberantly. The bride and bridegroom are instructed to sit cross-legged with the groom's left knee resting on the bride's right knee, symbolizing the submission of wife to husband. The groom rests his left hand in the palm of the bride's right hand to symbolize her commitment to serve as the bulwark of the family and to work hard for her husband and children.

Around midnight, the drum dancers enter the house, shouting and stomping their feet. The house vibrates with the pounding of their drums. The dancers circle the center post three times, then dance before the bride and groom. At some weddings the bride, groom, and the bridal party dance around the center post also and then resume their seats, but most houses are too small to permit such large processions. On completion of their dance, the drummers sit next to the center post and remain there until an elder from the bridegroom's lineage steps forward and strews flowers before them in thanks. They are presented a token gift of money and asked to bring joy to the wedding through music-making and dancing. The guests roar approval and the dancers file out the doorway together into the courtyard where they continue dancing until daybreak.

The shaman meanwhile resumes his chant of the myths and sings of the origins of the world and mankind, the bride and groom, and the happy home that they will build. No two shamans chant alike; we saw one sit before a bottle of liquor, praise the qualities of the brew, and describe how Limbus learned how to distill liquor and make beer. This lasted half an hour while the bride and groom sat silently amid the uproarious laughter of the guests. Guests wander through the house, fall asleep in the corners, join the drum dancers in the courtyard, and perhaps, if young and eligible, begin a rice dance outside.

Sometime between midnight and 3:00 A.M. a cock and hen are brought into the house and placed before the shaman, who sits in front of the bride and groom. The shaman holds one fowl in each hand and addresses the bride and groom, instructing them to remain faithful to each other and to obey the rules of Limbu marriage. He then kills the cock and hen by breaking their backs with a stick. In their last gasps for breath, the fowls spurt blood from their beaks. This blood is caught in a container made of leaves placed before the bride and groom. The shaman divines the blood and almost invariably predicts a happy and prosperous marriage with many children. The fowls are plucked and cooked, and morsels are offered to all the guests. The divination of the fowls climaxes the Limbu wedding ceremony. The bride and groom often doze off while the guests continue reveling until morning, but they are frequently wakened by the teasing and laughter of the visitors.

At sunrise, the guests gather in the courtyard for the final marriage ritual. The bride is asked to rise and is handed a broom for cleaning the house and sweeping the courtyard. She picks up a large clay or brass water jug and a carrying basket and, accompanied by her female in-laws, walks to the nearby spring to fetch water, a daily custom of Limbu women. She assists in cooking the morning meal and through these acts of servitude demonstrates her willingness to work hard for her husband and her in-laws.

In the final stage, the musicians of the tailor caste begin to play their instruments. A rug is spread on the ground in front of the house and the bride and groom sit side by side as before. The shaman squats in front of them and begins to instruct them again in the duties and obligations of marriage. He now takes a bit of unhusked rice from a brass bowl and hands it to the groom, who gives it to the bride. She rises, faces her husband, kneels and touches his feet with her forehead, then sits beside him. The groom is told never to take another bride nor to lie with another woman from this day forward. The bride is admonished to adhere to her marriage vows and remain faithful to her husband, who has paid the brideprice and will be her provider. The guests murmur their approval and the ceremony is completed. The tailor caste musicians offer their blessing by playing and dancing for the new husband and wife, and are rewarded by coin-throwing guests.

Some guests stay to eat meat and rice before returning home, while others are exhausted from the wedding festivities and leave early. The intermediator and the patrilineal relatives of the bridegroom slaughter a pig for the bride's parents. If they live far away, money is sent instead of meat, which might spoil. After the morning meal the bridal party, accompanied by the intermediator, departs for home with gifts of liquor, beer, meat, rice, and money.

The bride might return with the bridal party to her natal home and receive her husband there only occasionally until she has given birth to a child; more often she remains in her husband's home for two or three weeks after the wedding. But rarely will she stay permanently in her husband's home until she has given birth to her first child. The distance separating the couple's homes, the kinship ties the bride has in her husband's village, her age, and the tensions, real or imagined, with her new in-laws—all these factors influence if and when she stays with her husband. Their importance cannot be overstressed because they are the keys to understanding Limbu marriage stability.

## Life Cycle Rituals

All Limbus celebrate the three major events of the life cycle: birth, marriage, and death. Several other rites relevant to one or the other sex are nonobligatory and depend upon the family's wealth or the degree to which they have adopted Hindu customs. These include the "first rice-eating ceremony," the "first haircutting ceremony," and the "stomach ceremony" held during pregnancy. Women are, however, considered polluting to men during menstruation and directly after childbirth. Formalities surrounding a birth celebrate and purify both the infant and the mother. But men are the center of attention at only one ceremony, that of birth.

Several Limbu women told us the best time to conceive is the first day after a woman's period ends. Inside her stomach, they say, is a folded "baby putting place," which contains a piece of "flesh." If this "flesh" is met by the man's "pus" on the day she washes to remove menstrual pollution, a baby will grow and so will the "baby putting place." A child is thought to be in the womb for ten months, because pregnancy is marked from the first month menstruation ceases. If the pregnant woman is nursing another child at the time of conception, her milk usually dries up after three or four months. At about five months, she starts to crave sweets and other delicacies. The Limbu feel that a woman must work hard while she is pregnant to become strong enough for childbirth. When she becomes too ungainly to do heavy work, she can still lift loads of unhusked rice and other grains.

During the ninth month, pregnant women are the subjects of a ceremony to insure mother and unborn child a safe delivery and to protect them during the first months after the birth. This "stomach ceremony" has two stages—a set of sacrifices performed in daylight in the forest to give strength to the woman in labor, and a ritual that takes place at night in the woman's natal home. The Limbu believe that women who die in childbirth or children who die before they reach the age of two, become evil spirits who are given to attacking close women relatives in childbirth and newborn infants. The victim of such an attack sickens and sometimes dies. During the "stomach ceremony," shamans try to trap these spirits and bar them from harming mother or child.

A neighbor described the ceremony for us. The pregnant woman, her family and two shamans enter the jungle in the morning before eating rice, and there offerings are made to eight different deities. The first shaman offers one egg and a pair of fish to the god of fire, asking for strength during childbirth. Warokma Sammang, a large water pond deity, is then given one rooster, one hen, ten oil candles, ten leaf plates filled with tiny fried bread, four pairs of tiny bamboo containers filled with fermented grain and water, and four pairs of dried fish. The offering is elaborate because during the sixth month of pregnancy that deity has taken one of the woman's souls (the Limbu believe every person has seven souls). If the water pond god cannot be persuaded to give back the stolen soul, the woman will die in labor.

The animals are cut, and the shaman begs the deity to return the soul. Warokma Sammang replies that he cannot unless his friend Kontsokma Sammang is pacified as well. An offering is then presented to this deity: one egg-laying hen is released in the jungle. After this, the woman's soul is released. Lesser offerings are made to five more deities whom the shaman asks to grant the woman strength, health, and an easy labor.

When all the prescribed deities have been duly approached, the meat, rice, and liquor are prepared and served to everyone. Then the shaman holds out the woman's shawl and calls to her soul, "Come with us and we'll take you home. Where have you gone? Where have you been? What trouble have you suffered?" The soul replies, "I've suffered a lot, and no one came to take me back." When he hears of the soul's hardships the shaman weeps and says, "We didn't see you leave. Yesterday we said to come, but we didn't see the road. Now we've come to take you. Get up, now, let's go." The soul enters the woman's shawl and the priest puts it into a basket, covers it with the rest of her shawl, and carries it home, accompanied by all those present. When they reach her house, the shaman places the basket on a rug and tells the soul, "We have come; now sit, baby."

We found out about this ritual quite by accident. One afternoon we heard shouting in front of our house and saw two Limbu shamans stopped by the local police. Our cook explained that they were returning from a ceremony in the woods performed for a pregnant woman, but the police thought they were drunk. The pregnant woman, who was staying nearby at her mother's house, regularly visited our house and our cook fed her yogurt and eggs because she was pregnant. The woman's mother came into our kitchen after the police had gone and invited us to her house that night to witness the remainder of the ceremony.

We arrived at the old woman's house at 9:00 in the evening. The two shamans, one other Limbu man and relatives of the pregnant woman were already there. The shamans were building an elaborate altar atop a mound of dirt two feet in diameter behind the house. First a fence of small bamboo sticks was placed around the back and sides of the mound. A ladder, made of two bamboo sticks three feet high with three bamboo steps connecting them, was stuck in the middle of the mound, which was covered with a number of ritual objects.

The shaman in charge announced that his soul would "go up" the ladder, carrying the mother's soul along. He would "bring back down" the ladder not only the mother's soul, but also the unborn child's. When we asked him how he would find the baby's soul, he replied, "I can't say. I must look here and look there."

When the altar was completed, one of the shamans picked up a drum and his assistant lifted up a brass plate. Beating on these instruments, they danced into the house to make an offering to the house deity. Then they came outside and circled the mud mound for forty-five minutes, chanting Limbu scriptures. At intervals one shaman would blow on rice in his hand and scatter it on the ground as an offering. At the conclusion of this performance we were all served beer and a snack of cooked chicken by the women of the house while the two exhausted shamans rested.

The pattern of dancing and then resting was repeated twice. It was very late and we were growing sleepy. Suddenly the principal shaman began to growl. He picked up a dog's skull that had been lying on the altar wrapped in a white cloth, put it in his mouth, and jumped around on all fours, sniffing, growling, and yelping. He even chased after a dog, running on all fours into the fields surrounding the house.

The women were afraid and asked if we were also. This was part of the ritual, but their fear seemed real. They said the shaman was hunting spirits of children who died before the age of two, specifically, two dead girls of the pregnant woman's mother. If they were left to roam, they might attack her or her baby during birth.

When the shaman returned, still on all fours, he began leaping around the mound. He ran up to the pregnant woman, bent down, and began to "bite" her lower abdomen with the dog's skull. This went on for several minutes, then he "bit" her young son and several young girls, throwing the head away, looking at it, then picking it up again after each "bite." Suddenly he announced, "finished," asked for water to drink, and threw up.

We asked our cook if the shaman's soul would go up the ladder soon, and she replied that it was "up" at that very moment. When we asked if he was a dog when he danced with the head, she replied, "A dog's spirit was in his skin." After a while the shaman became calm, drank some liquor, and both shamans beat their instruments again. The principal shaman whistled softly and walked slowly to a shallow hole, dug near the house by his assistant during a break. Several women of the household had gathered there already. Suddenly the shaman threw a stick in the hole, the pregnant woman's mother threw in some live coals, and she and the shaman stamped on them, covering them with dirt.

Another long break occurred. Liquor and beer were served, and the two shaman talked and sang. The helper led the dancing for the first time, but he was very drunk and fell off the porch. When our cook tried to help him up, he screamed at her. Then he stopped and everyone laughed nervously. It was 3:45 in the morning and the ceremony was over.

The next day we questioned our cook about the ceremony. The two evil spirits had not been killed, as cow's milk would have been necessary to bring that about and none was available. They had been driven off, however, and a "fence was built" to keep them away from the baby. One of the pregnant woman's relatives who had died in childbirth had been "killed," because she could have killed the pregnant woman merely by touching her. Our cook did not know if the child's soul had "come down the ladder" with the shaman, but neighbors told us that after the ceremony the shaman would know the sex of the unborn child.

When a woman goes into labor, all men must be chased out of the house so that she will not "be embarrassed." Two or three women stay in the room during labor, one of whom acts as a midwife and should be an elderly relative of the pregnant woman. The midwife supports the woman during the birth, cuts and ties the umbilical cord, and supervises the bathing of the baby.

Once labor begins, the pregnant woman must sit up at all times to keep the baby from turning the wrong way inside the womb. One informant told us about a woman from a nearby village who always lay down in labor; as a result, all of her children came out of the womb in the wrong position and died. If a woman dies in pregnancy or childbirth, her stomach must be cut open and the baby pulled out. To prevent the baby being "too high," pregnant Limbu women bind themselves with their waistbands, and during labor they hang on to a pole and try to force the baby downward with another woman standing by to press on the stomach and to pull the baby out when it emerges.

When the afterbirth is expelled, a silver rupee must be placed on the cord, next to the baby. The midwife then cuts the cord with a bamboo knife and the mother names the baby, saying, "From now on you are my son [or daughter]." The time of birth is noted and, in a month or two, a ritually appropriate name will be given to the baby by a Brahman priest.

Immediately after the baby's cord is cut, it is tied by the midwife with string made of triple thread for a girl, quadruple thread for a boy. The baby is then washed by its mother (as it is covered with the blood of childbirth, it would be sinful if anyone else washed it), put to the breast, and lulled to sleep. Unless there are complications, no shaman is needed.

The afterbirth must be put in a bamboo container and tied high in a tree by the midwife. The tree's bark must be cut with a knife to see if white sap comes out; if it does, mother's milk will be plentiful. Three loops of the bamboo strip are used as ties for a girl, and four loops for a boy; then the tree is shaken, three times for a girl and four times for a boy. This procedure prevents the child from throwing up its mother's milk and dispels fears in later life.

After the birth, the mother is rubbed all over her body with clarified butter, and oil and butter are combed through her hair. That night, liquor is brewed and she sits near the fire to sweat and prevent illness. She must be rubbed down with butter for at least two or three days thereafter. Moreover, for one month after the birth she will be fed hot butter, chicken, beer and liquor, but no yogurt or very hot foods.

Sexual intercourse is permitted up until the time of birth, but after the birth, Limbu women insist a woman should not sleep with her husband for seven to fifteen days lest the "baby putting place" fall out and cause sterility. If the new mother eats good food and refrains from intercourse for the proper time, the "place" will shrink and return to its original position.

The baby is rubbed down daily to prevent illness and put to sleep in a rag-filled wicker basket which swings from the ceiling. When a cradle is first made, the project must be completed in one day. The first time the cradle is used, a broom must be put inside and rocked, then a dog, then a cat. After that, the baby can be placed inside, and the same cradle is used for all successive children in the family.

New mother and child must remain inside the house several days, three days after the birth of a girl and four days after the birth of a boy. During this time the new mother must lie in a corner on straw. Other women come to visit and drink beer during this period of seclusion, but because the house is ritually polluted by the blood of childbirth, men may not be served food or drink inside.

At the end of this period, a "bathing ceremony" purifies the house. Nearby relatives gather "when the cock crows," and mother, baby, and midwife must bathe and put on clean clothes. The midwife covers the floor with a new layer of mud, cow dung, and water, and sprinkles cow urine over it. All the women who are present must drink a little of the cow urine.

After this purification, the new mother puts rice and vegetables on the fire, saying, "From today on, it is all right to eat my food again." She presents the midwife with a new blouse and one rupee, and puts a blessing on her forehead. Each of the guests places a blessing on the baby's forehead, and everyone has beer, liquor, rice, vegetables, and meat.

Babies are breast-fed until they are four or five months old. If the family can afford it, the infant's first solid food is celebrated by a "first rice-eating ceremony." In wealthy families, the services of a Brahman priest are required; poorer families conduct the ceremony without a priest. The child is fed rice and other food by its mother, father, and mother's brother, and receives gifts of money. Limbu women said that if this ceremony could not be performed for all their children, they prefer it for boys. A third childhood ritual, the "first haircutting ceremony," is for boys only, usually when they reach the age of five.

Except for the marriage ceremony, no rites signify the passage of Limbu girls and boys from adolescence to adulthood. No special observances mark a girl's first menstruation, although other caste groups such as the Newar do have such ceremonies. Limbu girls are extremely embarrassed by the onset of their menses, often do not tell their mothers, or may even deny that they are menstruating. Although menstruating women can socialize with and serve food to other women, it is "sinful" for them to serve food to men. (Several Limbu women, however, confided that their husbands would eat the food they prepared while menstruating if there were no other women in the house to cook and serve it.) If a shaman, either male or female, eats food prepared by a menstruating woman, he or she will become "possessed." Menstruating women are also prohibited from touching or reading books, and from having sexual intercourse. After three or four days, the woman must wash herself and her clothes thoroughly and may then resume all normal activities.

Rituals surrounding the death of a Limbu symbolize the value of male-female differences not only in the behavior of the participants but in the particulars of the ceremonies. The death of a Limbu requires that two rites be performed, a funeral and a wake. The funeral usually takes place the day after death, and, except for wealthy Limbu who cremate their dead, comprises rituals which take place when the corpse is buried in a graveyard. Only men are permitted to dig the grave, construct the rock slab coffin, and inscribe the gravestone. Women who attend sit on the outskirts of the graveyard while the grave is being dug; later, those who are members of the immediate family often gather about the grave, weeping.

Funeral rites are conducted by a shaman in three stages and women are only permitted to remain through the first two. At the end of the second stage, when the dead person had been placed in the ground, the shaman cries out, "This is not our house, this is a dead man's house. Those who love this person must leave." All the women scatter, and the men cover the grave and conclude the burial. When the women leave the graveyard, they must scrub their hands in fresh water with a plant which has ritual cleansing properties, then they are offered beer by women from the deceased person's family. The men at the funeral follow the same procedure when they have finished constructing the grave.

A period of mourning follows, ending with the wake or "day of weeping," when the deceased's spirit is given a last ritual meal and sent to the abode of the spirits. The length of the mourning period is three days after death for a woman, and four days after death for a man. If circumstances prevent the wake from being held on the prescribed day, a ritual period of mourning takes place for an appropriate time during which the sons of the deceased must "sit in a corner" on an upside-down red mat, naked except for a blanket, and observe taboos on eating and social interaction.

On the day of the wake, males play a dominant role whatever the sex of the deceased. Men of the family cook large pots of rice for the assembled guests and make paper flowers to be used in the ritual feast for the deceased spirit. The sons of the deceased must shave their heads and play a principal role in the ritual.

Certain of the themes that run throughout Limbu life cycle ceremonies indicate that males have a higher status than females in Limbuan. For example, in optional ceremonies such as the "first rice-eating," boys rather than girls are given preference; women in their menses and directly after childbirth are polluting to men, but not to other women.

But the significance of Limbu symbolism is not always as it seems to Western eyes. The association of women with the number three and men with the number four in the rituals surrounding birth and death indicates a clear-cut differentiation of status between males and females, to be sure, but not necessarily a superior/inferior differentiation. The requirement that someone must "sit in a corner" to remove pollution from the household after birth and after death affords some interesting insights. At the beginning of the life cycle—birth—it is a woman, the mother, who must "sit," while at the end of the life cycle—death—it is a man, the dead person's son. Symbolically, the rituals of birth and death highlight some basic principles underlying the relations between the sexes in Limbuan and the significance attached to each sex. Women, who "sit in a corner" at birth, are in fact viewed as the givers of life and symbolize the life process; men, who "sit in a corner" at death, are the takers of life and symbolize the process of death. Only men hunt and fish, only men go to war and kill, and only men in Limbu society are allowed to kill or slaughter animals for food. Only women give birth and nourish the infant into childhood and puberty.

100

# Case Histories of Marriage Problems

## 5

A true understanding of Limbu marriage and divorce is probably better gained from actual case histories than from a series of statistics. Divorce data in small-scale societies are extremely unreliable as indicators of marriage stability, particularly in societies like the Limbu where marriage is a gradual process rather than a clear-cut legal act. Cold statistics do not help us to understand fully the background of marital situations, nor do they reveal the context in which marriage takes place. Many societies do not permit divorce, yet marriages in those communities may be as fragile and unstable as in those with high divorce rates. The following case studies reflect a range of marital situations that can tell us a great deal not only about the probable causes of separation and divorce but also about the ingredients that go into a successful mariage.

*1: Elopement*   Most Limbu marriages follow a pattern from courtship through arranged negotiations between the families by the bridegroom's intermediator. Brideprice is agreed upon, a wedding date is set, and the couple are formally betrothed at the bridegroom's home. The following story illustrates a different type of marriage—a type that shows the flexibility of Limbu values concerning marriage as well as some of the attitudes and concerns of uninvolved friends. It was told to us by a young girl of eighteen years, and it concerns events that took place the year before we arrived in Limbuan.

A sixteen-year-old girl from a village near the Tehrathum Bazaar eloped with a Limbu policeman who worked for the Nepal central government. His home was somewhere near Mewa Khola, about three days' walk to the north. The couple had danced on several occasions while he was stationed in Tehrathum Bazaar and one day he took the girl to his home without notifying anyone. Her mother found out, visited his home, and told her daughter, "From now on you are this man's wife and you should act like a wife." No brideprice was given, nor were any gifts exchanged.

Listeners agreed that nothing could be done about the elopement, since the girl was unmarried. But another person said, "This is the way people act these days; they give no brideprice, no gifts. The girl will probably run off with another man soon." Others agreed that would be the probable outcome, given the circumstances. The storyteller announced that she would never elope because she would lose face with her parents and relatives. Although everyone agreed that the marriage was legitimate, none favored elopement. Many thought that the marriage was doomed because of the man's failure to establish good relations with the girl's natal kinsmen through gift exchanges. The discussants agreed that the boy should present bridewealth payments to stabilize the situation.

Under normal circumstances, the girl's parents never visit their son-in-law's home until after the couple have a child. In this elopement situation, the in-laws visited often; however, the man was not living in his father's homestead.

*2: Widowhood and Remarriage*  A widow or a widower who remarries still maintains certain ties to the kinsmen of the deceased spouse, as illustrated in this example.

A man living near Tehrathum Bazaar married a woman from a village about two hours' walk away and paid a brideprice of 180 rupees plus bridewealth payments. The couple had a daughter but the wife died shortly after childbirth, and the child was raised for a while in her mother's village. Her father served in the army for twelve years before he quit because his regiment was transferred to India. On his return to Limbuan he married a widow from Cathar province who spoke a different dialect and lived over a day's walk away. (Her first husband had died shortly after marriage.) At the time of our initial field work the couple had been married almost ten years and had a daughter of their own. No brideprice had been paid in this marriage and the annual bridewealth payments were completed. The husband visited his wife's natal home many times with gifts of meat and liquor, and his relationship with his in-laws was excellent. He also visited his dead wife's natal home frequently, and his first daughter alternated between living at her father's house and at the natal home of her deceased mother.

Widow remarriage is approved among Limbus, and in this case the second union was apparently marred only by the fact that it had failed to produce sons. The man complained to us that he was being "witched" since he had no heirs. He blamed witchcraft rather than his present wife for the problem, however, and never thought of taking a second wife to rectify the situation.

*3: Co-wives Fight* This case describes a polygynous marriage that began with the approval of the first wife but deteriorated into an open conflict between co-wives.

The cousin-brother of the widower of Case History 2, whose home is within the same homestead, married a woman who lived in a village across the river, about one day's walk away. A brideprice of approximately 100 rupees was given, and annual bridewealth payments were duly made. The woman came to live with him approximately two years after the wedding ceremony. At the time of our acquaintance, they had been married eleven or twelve years and had one daughter but no sons. After three or four years of marriage, the woman urged her husband to take a second wife inasmuch as she had conceived no more children and apparently could not produce a son as heir. The husband agreed, and married a woman near Chainpur. He paid a small brideprice and completed the bridewealth payments. The two wives lived together in their husband's home for three or four years, during which the second wife produced no children. Meanwhile, to complicate an already tense situation, the wives began to argue and eventually the second wife moved back with her family. The man by now loved his second wife deeply, and this increased the anxieties and jealousies of the first. Three years before our initial field work, the man took a permanent government job at Taplejung and his second wife went there to live with him. On his periodic visits to his home in Limbuan, he had to listen to the complaints of his first wife. The Limbu of the area were fond of citing this situation as an example of what happens when a man takes two wives.

By 1975 the man had lost his job in Taplejung and returned to his home with his second wife. The two wives now live together, but the first wife completely dominates the household. The second hardly ever speaks out, and seems to have given way entirely to the wishes of the first. The man frequently refers to the second wife, who still has produced no children, as "crazy" and "dumb." Seven years have tempered the flames of love.

*4: The Adulterous Wife*   This case is somewhat atypical of adulterous *(jāri)* marriages in that no compensation was paid to the former husband, but it demonstrates the importance of gift exchange. The marriage in question is unstable because it has not produced children and because the wife has a history of infidelity.

The nephew of one of the parties of Case History 3 lives in a house with his father, his wife, and his father's brother and *his* first wife and their daughter. First married by arrangement to a woman of an unknown clan, he paid a brideprice of 150 rupees and a substantial first bridewealth payment, but his bride ran away to Assam with another Limbu before she came to live in his home. Since he was unable to make the journey to Assam to collect compensation, he received nothing and the girl's parents refused to refund the brideprice.

He met his present wife at a dance in Mewa Khola province, about three day's walk away, when she was married to another man. The neighbors confirm that she had two or three husbands before her present marriage and therefore has a history of run-away marriages. She and her present husband "fell in love" while dancing and he took her to his home. Neighbors say he paid no compensation because she had a reputation as a "loose" woman.

Shortly after the second marriage, the husband sent a substantial bridewealth payment of a water buffalo, liquor, and clothes to the wife's parents. He also made regular annual payments. The couple had been married over two years at the time of our initial field work, but had no children. The man was threatening to take a second wife and conducting amorous adventures at courtship dances.

The woman threatened to leave him if he took a second wife. The bridewealth from her first marriage enabled her parents to give her fine clothes and gold and silver jewelry. By Limbu standards she was wealthy, somewhat independent, and envied by the other women of the homestead. Both of her husband's parents were dead (her father-in-law died while we lived in Limbuan) and the women in her husband's household had little, if any, control over her actions. The marriage was relatively unstable and many people secretly believed it would eventually dissolve. The husband, however, hoped to save the marriage because the girl and her parents were wealthy.

104

Seven years later, however, Rex observed no change in the marriage. The couple still had not produced children, but the husband had not made good his threats to take a second wife. Although the woman at that time constantly bemoaned the fact that she had reached the age of 40 years without a child, her personal wealth had increased tremendously, and her husband apparently considered her wealth adequate compensation for the lack of an heir.

*5: Running Away and Forcing an Issue*   The procedure of divorce is illustrated in this case as well as the urge to conform to the ideal marriage pattern of two sisters of one clan marrying two brothers of another clan.

Three or four years ago, a girl of Chathar province married, by arrangement, a man from a village near Tehrathum. A substantial brideprice and bridewealth payments were made. Her parents insisted that the girl move to live with her husband shortly after the wedding ceremony. The husband was kind and generous to his young wife, but she did not like him and fought constantly with her in-laws. The failure of the marriage to produce children only added to the tensions.

One day toward the end of our field work, the girl visited her older half-sister (they had the same father but different mothers) in a village near to us. The older sister was a widow, had two children, and seemed relatively content with her lot. During the visit, the younger sister met her older sister's young brother-in-law. He had just returned from Assam where he had amassed considerable wealth—enough to retrieve some of his family's mortgaged lands. The runaway wife danced with this young man on several occasions and, according to our neighbors, "fell in love with him."

The older sister urged the girl to leave her present husband and marry the young man because "sisters should live together" and "both of us would be happier with the situation." Women from adjacent homesteads, including the young man's mother, also encouraged the match. Apparently the circumstances looked promising to the girl because the man was wealthy, his parents seemed quite agreeable, and she and her sister would live in the same household. She decided to marry him without returning to her former husband. A simple ceremony was held and the young man's relatives came to sanction the new marriage.

Two or three days later, the first husband came looking for his wife. Suspecting what had happened, he asked a man from the same clan as the new husband to accompany him and his brother-in-law on the trip from their village in Chathar province. When they reached the village where the couple were now living, he began to beat his former wife but was stopped by his brother-in-law and his companion. The companion urged the man to go home and seek *jāri* compensation, and he promised to help mediate.

The next day, the first husband's father visited the mediator and demanded that his son be paid 1,000 rupees compensation, in accordance with Nepali law. The mediator delivered the message to the *jāri* husband's household, but he refused to pay, so the adulterer's mother was asked to persuade him. She refused to listen to the mediator. Finally, the mediator wrote to the *jāri* woman's younger brother in Chathar province, asking him to come and help.

A week later, several people met at the mediator's house: the *jāri* woman's younger brother and the chief of her natal lineage, her first husband's father and the chief of his lineage, and the chief of the *jāri* husband's village. They eventually agreed that a sum of 650 rupees, or its equivalent in goods and livestock, should be paid to the aggrieved husband and a "promise of payment" paper was drawn up. Although no payment had been made by the time we concluded our field work, neighbors agreed that the man would be forced to pay if he hoped to stay married: public opinion and the influence of so many important people guaranteed compensation. If remuneration was not delivered, the first husband would go to court and send his rival to jail.

In "adulterous marriages," compensation is ordinarily paid only if the aggrieved husband can gather support from close relatives and influential people. In this instance, the husband avoided violence by bringing a man who had a reputation for fairness and was a relative of the *jāri* husband, to act on his behalf. If he had attempted to settle the matter himself, he might have killed the second husband. He did attempt to beat his wife but was restrained by the mediator who accompanied him. Through skillful negotiations and by consulting all those legitimately concerned, the mediator was able to secure an agreement in writing that had the sanction of prominent men from both sides.

Kinship connections played an important role in the negotiations. The mediator was married to a woman from Chathar province and could trace affinal alliances to the *jāri* girl's natal home. He belonged to the same clan as the *jāri* husband and was a close neighbor, which was crucial to the negotiations and to a fair settlement.

The case illustrates the importance of relationships with in-laws and the birth of children in keeping marriages on a firm footing. The girl left her first husband because of conflicts with her in-laws even though he was a kind and generous man. Had she had children, her marital situation might have been less irksome. The new marriage offered a chance to live in a wealthier household where she had close kinship ties through her sister, who had children and was well liked by her in-laws. The girl could only benefit from this marriage, and the positive reinforcement she received from the other women of the area confirmed her decision.

*6: The Reluctant Bride*   This case illustrates the reluctance of a young Limbu girl to move into her husband's household, and her parents' role in urging her fidelity before the move.

A man from a village near Tehrathum Bazaar took a wife from a village about a half-day's walk away. The marriage was by arrangement, and a brideprice of 180 rupees plus a substantial bridewealth payment was made. At the time of our initial field work the marriage was seven years old. The man was about twenty-five and the girl about twenty-two, and they had a three-year-old daughter. The couple were our neighbors during our stay and became good friends. Before we met them, they had lived one year in the man's father's house but conflicts between the wife and the mother-in-law forced them to leave. The girl now complained constantly about her mother-in-law, and we felt inclined to sympathize: it seemed the older woman was always at her door yelling at her to do some chore.

The girl had no relatives nearby, and the female half of our research team became her close confidante. She was willing to talk frankly to us about the intimacies of a Limbu marriage; indeed, she was the information source for several of these case histories.

As for her own marriage, she said she had had no sexual relations with her husband for the first two years. After the third and final bridewealth payment was made to her family she had attempted to live with her husband until intolerable conflicts with her mother-in-law forced her to return to her natal home, where she remained until the fifth year of marriage. She had threatened many times to run away with another man during those years but her parents prevented that by watching her closely. They were determined to see the marriage succeed. Shortly after the birth of her baby girl, she moved again into her husband's household.

Her husband treated her well and loved her very much. Her refusal to sleep with him in the early years of their marriage was attributable primarily to her age. She was only fifteen when they married and claimed she was "embarrassed." Her parents' understanding eventually helped her overcome her fear—and clearly that understanding was based on good in-law relations established through brideprice and the fulfillment of the marriage payments.

Seven year later, Rex found that the couple had four children—two boys and two girls. The mother-in-law moreover had moved into the home and occupied the lower floor. She no longer scolded and yelled at her daughter-in-law, however, for the younger woman, now mature, had established total control of the household and no one challenged her suzerainty. The couple had also come into considerable wealth, by hill standards, owing to the fortunate location of their property. They had sold a portion of the land as a site for a large government building, and their location on the main bazaar road enabled the woman to realize a profitable income from the sale of home brew and liquor. The startling change in this family as a result of the children and an improved standard of living reveals a great deal about the factors that go into stabilizing a Limbu marriage.

*7: The Importance of Having Sons* The following case describes a stable marriage between a Limbu man and a girl from a neighboring ethnic group which shares a common cultural heritage. The most important stabilizing factor in this marriage was the birth of sons.

A Limbu male living near Chainpur Bazaar met a Yakha Rai girl neighbor at the rice dances and married her by arrangement. At the time of the wedding, he was about twenty-two years old, and she was eighteen. The exact amount of the brideprice was unknown, but was estimated at 120 rupees. The girl's family is believed to have received an acceptable bridewealth gift after the wedding as well as three years of payments.

The girl moved to live with her husband immediately after the wedding ceremony. Her village was nearby, so she did not have typical problems of adjustment and loneliness. One year after the wedding the couple had a baby boy and the girl later gave birth to three more boys, one of whom died at the age of two. The couple had been married eight years.

The marriage was very congenial even though the husband and wife spoke mutually unintelligible native languages. Nepali was their common tongue. The completion of gift exchanges, the birth of sons, and the acceptance of the girl by her in-laws contributed to the marriage's success.

*8: The Much-Married Man* It is not unusual for a long-lived Limbu male to have a number of marriages before he dies. This case history illustrates a number of the possible variations in Limbu matrimonial practices—widow remarriage, polygyny, divorce, marriage by arrangement, and "bride theft."

*108*

A man from a village near Chainpur had been married to five different women by the time we began our field work. He first joined the army when he was sixteen years old but left without a pension. When he returned from the British Gurkhas, he was married by arrangement to a Yakha Rai girl (the elder sister of Case History 7), who was only about fourteen years old. After two or three years of marriage without children, the man took a second wife, also a Yakha Rai girl, from a nearby village. The second wife had a daughter but never moved to live permanently with her husband. She conceived a second time and died in her natal home soon after the birth of a son. Conflicts between the two wives had prevented their happy coexistence.

Not long after the death of his second wife, the man's first wife died in childbirth. Before she died, however, the man took a third wife (Case History 12, a Limbu girl), for whom he paid 200 rupees in brideprice and presented a substantial bridewealth payment to the girl's parents. The third wife apparently lived with him only four months before squabbles with the first wife (who was now pregnant) drove her back to her natal home. Soon thereafter, she ran off with another man.

After the death of his first and second wives and the *jāri* marriage of his third, the man married a seventeen-year-old Limbu girl from a different village. A small brideprice was paid and a small wedding ceremony was held, followed by bridewealth payments to the girl's parents. The girl lived with him for approximately ten months and then died childless. (Death at a young age—either from accident or from diseases such as tuberculosis, dysentery, cholera, and smallpox—is a common occurrence in the rugged hill country of Nepal, where life is far more difficult than most outsiders can imagine. This particular girl died of tuberculosis.)

The man, now thirty-five years of age, then married a fifth time, to a nineteen-year-old Limbu girl. Again a brideprice was paid and a small ceremony held, and the initial bridewealth payment was made to the bride's parents. Shortly after the first annual bridewealth payment, the girl moved to live with him. By the time all payments were completed, the woman had given birth to five sons. This marriage was sturdy and, again, the birth of sons is the key stabilizing factor.

*9: The Company of Kinship*  The inclination to take wives who are related to the wives of patrilineal relatives is exemplified in this case, as are the stabilizing factors of gift exchange and children.

The younger brother of the man in Case History 7 married a girl from a distant village by arrangement, paid a small brideprice, and completed the annual bridewealth payments. The girl moved to live with him after the first year of marriage and eventually gave birth to three daughters, all of whom died before the age of five. The wife also died when she was about twenty-two years old.

After his wife died, the man married the younger sister of his elder brother's wife (the fifth wife of Case History 8). He was about twenty-seven years old then and the girl was not yet eighteen. A brideprice was paid, and the initial bridewealth gifts were given after a small ceremony. Since the girl's sister was already married to the man's elder brother, she moved into his household immediately. In the next seven years, she had four children—a boy and three girls. The boy died at the age of two.

Because the girl married into a family where she was able to trace close kinship ties and because her children were born in rapid succession, the marriage was stabilized.

*10: The Mother-In-Law Problem*   This case exemplifies clearly the instability of a Limbu marriage due to conflicts with the bride's mother-in-law. It also demonstrates how bridewealth and gift exchange induce the girl's parents to keep her from running away with another man.

A man from a village north of Tehrathum married, by arrangement, a girl from a nearby village, when he was about twenty-one and she was eighteen. Over 100 rupees in brideprice and a large bridewealth payment were made following a regular wedding ceremony. The girl attempted to live in the husband's household several times during the first three years of marriage, but each time quarrels with her mother-in-law precipitated her return to her natal home. The last time she stayed for nine years and only went back to live with her husband when her mother-in-law died.

Throughout those nine years, the girl threatened repeatedly to run off with another man, but her parents always stopped her. They pointed out that her husband was a good man, had paid a substantial brideprice, and had fulfilled his obligations to his in-laws through gifts. The girl meanwhile danced with other men, but always in the presence of her parents.

At the time of our field work, the girl had been living with her husband for two years and they had a one-year-old son. After years of instability and potential dissolution, the marriage was very successful.

*11: Too Many Marriages*   Once a woman divorces a man through *jāri*, she acquires a reputation, and repeated *jāri* marriages mark her as a rather "loose" woman. In extreme cases she may even be compelled by public opinion to leave Limbuan permanently, especially if no compensation has been paid. This case illustrates that principle.

The daughter of Case History 8 was married four times and eventually ostracized from Limbuan. She was first married at the age of fifteen to a village boy from Chathar province, about one day's walk from her natal home. A brideprice of 200 rupees was paid and a large expensive wedding ceremony was held. A substantial bridewealth payment was subsequently backed up by two years of annual payments. The girl moved into her husband's household shortly after the ceremony although his village was far away from her natal home and her relatives. They lived together two years, but she felt persecuted by her in-laws and her emotional vulnerability was complicated by her youth.

Soon she began to pay extended visits to her natal home, and eventually, after a dance, she moved into the home of a man living near her natal village. The man paid 500 rupees *jāri* compensation—one bull, some gold, and one large silver anklet. No wedding ceremony was held to honor the *jāri* marriage but one annual bridewealth payment was paid to the girl's parents. She lived with her second husband for one year.

While he was temporarily absent from home, she went to the bazaar in Athrai province for a fair and, after dancing with a local Limbu man, decided to leave her husband and stay there. No compensation was paid, and after lengthy negotiations the adulterer, fearing imprisonment by the police, fled with the girl to Assam in India.

After the couple reached Assam, where a number of Limbu have emigrated, the girl was attracted to a Limbu policeman and deserted her third lover. She and her fourth husband moved to Darjeeling, where they still live. No payment has been made in the last two marriages.

The Limbu describe the girl as a "whore" and say that only a fool would marry a woman who has been with so many men.

*12: The Co-Wife Problem*   Conflicts with co-wives are grounds for the dissolution of many a marriage. In this case history, the discrepancy in the couple's ages may have further contributed to the girl's decision to run away with another man.

A seventeen-year-old girl living in a village near Chainpur contracted a marriage by arrangement with a thirty-four-year-old man (see Case History 8) from a nearby village. The man already had one wife, who at the time appeared unable to have children.

The young girl moved into the household immediately after a small ceremony and the payment of 200 rupees in brideprice. Although the initial bridewealth payment was made to the girl's parents, she left her husband before any annual payments could be presented. She lived with the man for four months but was unable to adjust to the demands of the first wife, who had finally become pregnant after many years of marriage. The second wife returned to her natal home for a visit and danced on several occasions with a Yakha Rai of a nearby village, decided not to return to her husband, and took up residence with her lover. A *jāri* settlement of 600 rupees was decided upon. She still lives with the second husband in a stable marriage and has children, but details are missing. It was uncertain if bridewealth payments has been given to the girl's parents by the second husband.

*13: The Stress of Separation*   Young Limbu men are a highly mobile lot. Most of the more adventurous ones try to join the British Gurkhas, and if they are rejected they often journey to Darjeeling, Assam, or other parts of India to "seek their fortune," involving themselves in a number of love affairs along the way before returning home for a proper marriage. Even the less venturesome males are commonly forced by land shortages and economic pressures to emigrate to India or southern Nepal for temporary work and enough cash to retrieve mortgaged lands or pay bridewealth. Long-term separation of husband and wife because of labor migration is a variable in Limbu marriage stability of extreme importance to this study. This example, as well as that of Case History 19, describes some of the problems between spouses attributable to long- term separation.

A man from a village near Chainpur spent some time working in Ilam district during his late teens and early twenties to earn money to retrieve some of his family's mortgaged lands and to pay for a wife. In Ilam he lived with a Rai girl, but paid no brideprice and did not have a wedding ceremony. They lived together a year and she died childless. Eventually he returned to his village with a little cash and retrieved some of the mortgaged land. He thereupon arranged a marriage with a girl from a village near Mewa Khola province and paid a brideprice and the initial bridewealth. She moved into his home soon after the wedding ceremony and gave birth to a son. Annual bridewealth payments were made and the couple eventually had two more sons and five daughters. One of the sons and three of the daughters died before they were five years old. (The oldest son of this marriage is described in Case History 14, and the oldest daughter in Case History 15.)

Economic problems eventually forced the man to move to Assam, where he lives now with the two youngest children. His wife still lives in his home with their oldest son and his family. The person who told us this story says that the man left his home "because of the death of his other children," but it should be noted as well that his land is clearly insufficient to support his growing family. Gossip has it that the man "sleeps around," but the marriage itself does not appear to be in trouble and he visits his family often.

*14: The High Costs of Compensation*  Collecting adultery compensation can be a matter of vital importance to an aggrieved husband of limited means because it can enable him to contract a second marriage. The compensation rarely covers all the expenses of brideprice, wedding ceremony, and initial bridewealth payments, however. The heavy marriage expenses incurred twice by the man in this case, who is the son of the couple of Case History 13, may have contributed to his father's decision to move to Assam.

The man first contracted a marriage by arrangement with a girl from a nearby village, paid 150 rupees as brideprice and a substantial bridewealth gift of meat and liquor. Exact wedding expenses of the wedding are unknown, but it was a lavish ceremony. The girl never took up permanent residence in her husband's household, and broke her marriage contract seven months later by moving to live with a man from a nearby village (possibly a former rice dance partner). Although the adulterer paid compensation valued at 450 rupees in the form of 150 rupees cash, one silver coin, one gold necklace, and one gold nose pin, it was estimated that this amounted to less than two-thirds of the original wedding expenses.

After collecting compensation the man married a girl from another distant village, paid 200 rupees as brideprice and again held a small wedding ceremony and presented the initial gift to the girl's patrilineage. The second wife immediately came to live with him and within a year gave birth to a daughter. The husband has paid bridewealth annually and the marriage is stabilized.

*15: The Rewards of Paying Brideprice*  Failure to pay brideprice or *jāri* compensation and to legitimize a Limbu marriage through gift exchange seems to invite marriage instability, as this case shows.

A man from a village near Tehrathum ran away with another man's wife from a distant village after they danced at her natal home. He refused to pay adultery redress, and after they had lived together for six months she ran off with another man (see Case History 16).

The man apparently learned from his first experience not to expect something for nothing, for he then arranged a match with a girl from a nearby village (the eldest daughter of Case History 13) and this time paid 300 rupees in brideprice—more than the average—and a large initial bridewealth payment. The girl, only fourteen at the time of the wedding ceremony, lived with her mother and her brother's family until the three years' payments were complete. The large brideprice and the generous marriage payments prompted the girl's parents to encourage her to remain faithful. She recently moved to live with him after giving birth to a daughter who died in infancy. The marriage is relatively stable because the wife finds her in-laws agreeable and because her natal home is nearby—but there can be little doubt that the husband's conscientious payments helped the situation. The demand of a high brideprice may have resulted from her brother's exorbitant marriage expenses (see Case History 14) and the need to save her family from near destitution.

*16: The Sullied Woman*  The damaged standing of a woman who has repeatedly been involved in *jāri* marriage is detailed in this case. The role of brideprice and *jāri* compensation in shoring up marriage stability is also indicated.

The first wife of Case History 15 was married to a man from a nearby village after payment of a small brideprice of 80 rupees and token bridewealth. After the wedding, she lived with her husband for two years until constant bickering with her in-laws made her return to her natal home. There, at a dance, she met the man who became her second husband. The second husband refused to pay *jāri* compensation to the first husband, and the new marriage seems to have ended abruptly because the girl once more was unable to accept her in-laws. Within six months she ran away again—with a man from Mewa Khola province. Again no compensation was paid, nor did the third husband offer bridewealth payments to the girl's family. The couple lived together for almost four years, but their failure to have children convinced the man to take a second wife. He now claimed that the adulteress "was married too many times" and that he wanted a virgin bride. He married a second woman by arrangement and paid 130 rupees in brideprice plus bridewealth. His second wife moved to live with him and now has a baby girl. Relations are strained between the co-wives, and neighbors think the adulteress will take up with another man if the opportunity arises.

*17: The Promiscuous Man*  Male promiscuity does not seem to be as important a factor in fostering Limbu marriage instability as female promiscuity. In Case History 16, the woman's "infidelity" drew her into one marriage after the other, but in this case, a man's open indiscriminate behavior did have the same effect. Admittedly, this example is atypical in at least two ways: the man took a second wife simply as a "lover" and not because his first wife was barren; and, the man's mother sided protectively with his first wife, who had given birth to many children and apparently worked hard in the home.

The man was a native of a village about one day's walk from Tehrathum. He arranged a marriage with a girl near Tehrathum Bazaar, paid a brideprice of 100 rupees, and completed *all* marriage payments including the final one. The couple had been married for over nine years at the time of our field work, and because the brideprice payments were finished the girl had lost all legal connections to her natal home. She had moved to live with her husband shortly after the wedding ceremony and had a good relationship with her mother-in-law. She gave birth to a son after two years of marriage and then two daughters.

The man, however, had a reputation for promiscuity because over the years he had brought many girls home after the dance. His mother's usual reaction was to "chase them away" and scold her son, but his wife remained both passive and faithful. Recently he took a second wife, a young seventeen-year-old girl from a poor family, for whom he paid no brideprice or bridewealth. She moved in with him out of necessity, and seems intent on remaining despite the animosity of the man's mother and the co-wife. The person who told us the story says the mother-in-law is always screaming at the new wife and forcing her to work hard at menial chores in the hope that she will take up with some other man.

*18: The Old Man and the Young Girl*   The following case describes the marriage of a very young girl to her dead sister's husband. Such a union is not common among the Limbu, and the extreme discrepancy in age between the couple in this case most certainly brought about the dissolution of the union.

The girl in this case was but seven years old when she was married by arrangement to a man over fifty years of age who had been married to her dead elder sister. The man had paid a brideprice, one initial payment, and one annual bridewealth payment for her elder sister. For the second sister he paid a small brideprice and had completed the annual bridewealth payment at the time of our field work. The young girl, however, never moved to live with him but remained at her home in a distant village. When she reached puberty she ran away with a young boy from a different village who paid 320 rupees as compensation to the old man.

The adulterer died soon after the marriage and the widowed girl married a man from another village in Mewa Khola province. Because she proved unable to produce children, he eventually took a second wife, who lives in her natal home. Despite the first wife's barrenness and reputation as an adulteress, her third marriage appears stable, although conflicts with the co-wife may lead to trouble.

*19: Too Much Family Togetherness*  Labor migration sometimes creates unstable marriages because of long-term separations. In the following case, the wife's infidelity during her husband's absence was a reason for divorce. This case is particularly interesting in that the woman chose to have an adulterous relationship with a man who would be a likely potential for marriage if her husband died: her husband's younger brother. The adulterous behavior developed out of a strong joking relationship between the woman and the younger brother, a common situation in Limbu affinal relations.

A man from a village near Tehrathum Bazaar married a girl from a distant village. A brideprice and bridewealth were paid, and the couple had one daughter. When after some five years of marriage it became obvious that the man was unable to make a living on his land because of debts, he decided to go to Assam to acquire cash and retrieve some of his mortgaged lands. While he was away, his wife openly slept with his younger bachelor brother. Their adultery was known to all the neighbors and to the man's mother as well.

When the husband returned from Assam he discovered his wife was pregnant and it was not long before he learned the whole story. He went "crazy"—cut the house posts, broke plates, pottery, and other household utensils, and railed for days at his mother for having allowed such a dreadful thing to happen. His brother fled to India, fearing for his life. The mother, who was a widow, moved back to her natal home. The cuckolded husband sold all his animals and returned to Assam, taking his daughter with him. The mother thereupon returned to the house and kicked the adulterous daughter-in-law out. She went to her natal home and gave birth to a son, who recently returned on his own to his father's home, and now lives with a relative in that village. The mother went to Chainpur after the son left her and married a Yakha Rai. She died shortly after her second marriage, without having any more children.

The divorced husband is still unmarried but occasionally returns to his village to look after his property, now occupied by his mother and his younger brother's wife and children. The younger brother also returns

116

sometimes but avoids meeting his older brother because, people say, the man would kill him.

*20: The Good Marriages of Five Sisters*   The ideal Limbu marriage pattern is exemplified in this case of five sisters from a district south of our village. All five married men who were either relatives or close neighbors, which demonstrates how a system of kinship alliance through marriage can develop even between clans who live over two days' apart and speak different dialects.

Five sisters from a village in Panchthar province contracted marriages by arrangement to men from a village in Phedap province. In order of birth (using the Nepali designations) the sisters are Jethi (oldest), Mahili (second oldest), Kahili (third oldest), Sahili (fourth oldest), and Kanchi (youngest).

Jethi, who died a few years ago at the age of eighty, was the first of the sisters to marry. A high brideprice and bridewealth were paid and she moved to live with her husband in Phedap province within a year after the ceremony. Before the annual payments were completed, she gave birth to a daughter, and three years later she had a second daughter (both daughters contracted marriages with Yakha Rai men living near Chainpur Bazaar when they reached puberty). Jethi's marriage apparently was considered a model of success because all her sisters eventually followed her example.

Within a year after Jethi's marriage, Mahili, who is now eighty years old, married a man from a village less than two hours' walk away from her sister Jethi. A brideprice and bridewealth were paid and she too moved to her husband's village within a year after the wedding ceremony. Before the completion of annual payments, the birth of a son helped to stabilize the marriage. That son had two daughters, both of whom married brothers from the same clan in Athrai province.

Shortly after Mahili's marriage, Kahili's marriage was arranged with a man from the same village and clan. A large brideprice and marriage payment were paid and she moved to live with her husband almost immediately after the ceremony. She had four sons, the oldest of whom died at the age of sixteen, and three daughters, all of whom are married. (The oldest daughter is the fifth wife of Case History 8, and the youngest is the subject of Case History 6).

Sahili was the next to marry—she was wed by arrangement to the classificatory father's brother of Kahili's husband. Thus she lived in the same village as one of her sisters and close to two others. She moved into her husband's home immediately after the wedding ceremony and payment of the brideprice and eventually gave birth to several children, although only one son lived beyond the teen years.

Finally, the youngest sister, Kanchi, followed in the footsteps of all her sisters by marrying the classificatory younger brother of Mahili's husband. She lived next door to one of her sisters and within easy visiting distance of all the others. She is now forty-five years old. She gave birth to four daughters and five sons, but all four daughters died before the age of fifteen and three sons died before the age of ten. The two surviving sons are both in the British Gurkhas and unmarried.

The sisters' marriages were all stable even though all five married men who lived a great distance from their natal home. The endurance of these unions can be attributed primarily to kinship relations between the couples and the fact that the husbands' homes were near to one another.

*21: If at First the Marriage Fails, Try Again* After two unsuccessful attempts at marriage, a clan brother of the sisters in Case History 20 finally established a successful marriage with a girl from the sisters' area. This example describes the effects of separation and the instability of a polygynous marriage.

A man from a village in Panchthar province, now fifty-seven years old, took as his first wife a girl who was only fourteen. Her natal home was in a village near Tehrathum, and he paid a small brideprice and bridewealth. She never lived with him, claiming that his house was too far from her home and that she would be lonely without relatives nearby. After one year she ran off with a man from Chathar province with whom she had flirted at dances. Her first husband demanded her younger sister as a bride after he failed to receive *jāri* compensation. The younger sister was only eleven years old, but her parents agreed to the arrangement. When she reached puberty, however, she also ran off with another man, who died shortly thereafter without paying compensation. The girl returned to her natal home, and the jilted husband tried but failed to collect compensation from her parents.

Finally the man took a third wife from a village near where his clan sisters had married. He paid a large brideprice and bridewealth for his present wife, who was twenty-five years his junior. Today the couple have one son and twin girls, and the marriage appears successful. Recently he has taken his wife's younger classificatory sister (parallel cousin) as a second wife. His first wife agreed to the second marriage, but when the girl moved into the home, the co-wives began to argue. Despite their kinship relationship, the women could not live together, and the younger girl moved back to her natal home. She will probably look for another man soon.

*22: Family Spite and Legal Loopholes*   This case, like Case History 15, illustrates how crucial brideprice can be to a stable marriage. Failure to pay it can alienate even the most conscientious of in-laws and deprive the defaulter of strong allies. The case further demonstrates how dissatisfied parties on both sides of a marriage can use Nepali law to serve their own ends.

The eldest daughter of Case History 2 was married to a man from Chathar province whose clan and village are unknown. No brideprice was given, although the man sent a token initial bridewealth payment after the wedding ceremony and small gifts for two successive years. The girl repeatedly refused to move into her husband's household because she despised her mother-in-law. While she was living in the natal home of her dead mother (see Case History 2), her husband met another girl at a dance and took her as a second wife, hoping thereby to drive the first wife into a *jāri* marriage that would allow him to claim the adultery compensation to which he would then be entitled under Nepali law. He next paid a visit to his first wife's father and demanded that the girl move into his home immediately. The girl flatly refused, claiming she could not tolerate the presence of her mother-in-law, much less that of a strange co-wife. The girl's father, himself no stranger to current Nepali law, countered with a demand that the husband give his daughter a divorce "in writing" because bigamy had been declared illegal. The husband refused, saying that she would have to live with another man before he would divorce. At the end of our initial field work, the situation was unresolved but separation without compensation was indicated.

Seven years later, Rex met once again with the woman and her parents. The woman had married a second husband and borne him a son. The first husband had failed to collect *jāri* compensation because of the father's insistent citation of the new Nepali law forbidding polygyny.

The conclusion of this case points to the changes that are occurring in Limbu marriage as a result of edicts from the central government of Nepal. It also shows how those who are aware of these laws are able to manipulate them to their advantage in traditional Limbu marriage transactions.

Because the Limbu as a whole distrust all the agencies of Nepali government, such disputes are seldom argued in court; instead, the *threat* of recourse to the courts is used as leverage to hasten advantageous settlements. In this case, the father of the woman was able to foil her first husband's attempt to force a *jāri* settlement by asserting a counterclaim (the husband's plural marriage) and threatening to raise that counterclaim in a court of law.

# Divorce Limbu Style

# 6

We have noted the changing role of the Limbu woman, her contributions to Limbu economy, her authority within the household, her covert and overt powers in the decision making process, and the ambiguous and often difficult situation of marriage in a patrilineally organized society. Nowhere is her role more active, however, than in the dissolution of a marriage. In this chapter we try to explain the part she plays in divorce.

A young unmarried Limbu girl is relatively free to court with a number of eligible males; as a young married woman, her freedom is sharply curtailed by time-consuming new responsibilities and meddling in-laws. This restraint is foreshadowed symbolically in the wedding ceremony and subsequent gift exchange. The Limbu woman truly undergoes a change of life at marriage, a rite of passage from carefree adolescence to subdued adulthood.

A young childless wife feels and experiences tremendous psychological pressure and emotional conflict. Familial love and affection are replaced by discipline, hard work, and loneliness in her husband's household. Social pressure forces her to honor the wishes of her in-laws, particularly her mother-in-law, who disciplines her harshly. In the early months of her marriage she is like a stranger in a foreign country, subject to culture shock and alienation. She lives in a "non-status" state until she becomes a mother and is accepted in her husband's household and village.

The social distance that separates a young Limbu wife from her husband and his family is further expressed in language. A married woman without children is addressed neither by name nor by a kinship term, but rather by the impersonal "you." When she is referred to in the third person, she is "the wife of so-and-so" and her individuality is submerged in her husband's personality and image.* She is no longer even referred to by her own order of birth, as she was before marriage, but by her husband's. For example, if a "first daughter" marries a "third son," she is then "third daughter" rather than "first daughter."

Given all these considerations, one might expect that the Limbu wife—especially the childless wife—would have little control over the fate of her marriage. Not so. The degree of stability in a Limbu marriage is virtually entirely dependent on the woman's ability and desire to maintain an enduring relationship.

*This matter of personal address bears some explanation. The Limbu, like many peoples in Nepal and elsewhere, are extremely reluctant to address anyone directly. A person's name is sacred; the utterance of it in public or in conversation is taboo and causes embarrassment and shame. More than once we were chastised for calling each other by our first names, especially since we were married and had no children. Familiarity between equals or peers of the same age and sex who are not related by kinship is discouraged, but public familiarity between a newly married couple amounts to sacrilege.

The Limbu use kinship labels such as "brother" or "sister" irrespective of actual or real kinship relationships. Older people address the young as "younger brother" or "younger sister," and youths call elders "older brother" or "older sister." Very old people are frequently "grandfather" or "grandmother," terms connoting respect but at the same time a degree of warmth that is not implied in the terms "brother" or "sister." There is a comfortable feeling between people separated by two or three generations. Children are addressed in much the same tone of authority as might be used in speaking to animals, but in words that connote parental love, compassion, and understanding. Children may be designated "little father" or "little mother," for example. The terms for father and mother, who are like gods, are synonymous with respect, authority, undying affection, and devotion. When the same names are applied to children, the meaning is affectionately ironic. Children are "little animals," but at the same time "little gods."

The Limbu also refer to a person's order of birth. First-born sons are "oldest son," second-born sons are "second son," and so on. For daughters the pattern is the same, e.g., "oldest" daughter, "second" daughter, or "third" daughter. Therefore, each person has a name according to his or her order of birth and these designations are acceptable substitutes for kinship terms. Once strangers become friendly, they adopt the latter form of speaking. It is perfectly acceptable to ask a new acquaintance, "What son or daughter are you?" to learn how to address that person in the future.

Until children are born, husband and wife address one another obliquely, not directly. If a husband wants his wife to remove a pot from the fire he might say, "The pot needs to be removed from the fire." After the birth of a child, the husband and wife call each other "the mother of my son," or, "the father of my son."

## The "Adulterous Marriage"

Few Limbu marriages end in separation because of a husband's reluctance to meet matrimonial obligations. On the contrary, of twenty-four marriages that ended in separation (gleaned from a total of 156 marriages recorded from genealogies), twenty-one were dissolved because of the woman's *jari* or "adulterous" marriage, and the remaining three resulted from the woman's adultery (without *jari* marriage) or her inability to withstand conflicts with members of her husband's household. One of the non-*jari* divorces was caused by the wife's affair with her husband's younger brother during the husband's absence (see Case History 19 in chapter 5). The other two resulted from conflicts between co-wives, one of whom returned to her natal home and eventually remarried.

When Rex returned to survey the married women of three villages in 1975, he discovered that 21 percent of the women were living in a *jari* marriage situation. All of those interviewed traced their divorce of the first husband to discontent with in-laws, especially the mother-in-law. These interviews also disclosed that the vast majority of those who divorced had experienced an entirely arranged marriage at a very young age, many as young as eleven or twelve years. Comparing these women with those who eloped in their first marriage, he learned that only one marriage by elopement had ended in divorce through a second *jari* marriage. About 15 percent of all first marriages in the survey began with elopements. Once again, in a Limbu marriage, it appears that when the woman has a choice and is able to exercise that choice, her marriage is relatively stable and less likely to end in divorce.

Caplan (1970:89) feels that a man's motive for "adulterous marriages" is to side-step the high costs of a first union. Marriage expenses are irrelevant to a woman, since she is not directly affected by an extravagant ceremony or annual gift payments. Her primary objective is to find a man who will treat her well and whose relatives are congenial. Thus men and women turn to a *jari* marriage for very different reasons.

Men do commit adultery, but that is not always grounds for separation because the Limbu accept a double standard. When a man is away from home, he is expected to be unfaithful to his wife. If his desire for another woman is strong enough, he may take her as a second wife in a polygynous marriage, which is an approved form of marriage by tradition if not by current Nepali law. The Limbu woman, on the other hand, has two options: to be satisfied with her situation or to run away with another man. If a husband chooses to take his lover as a second wife, his first wife may be forced into adultery. More often, marriages are dissolved for complex reasons centering around the woman's unhappiness with her mother-in-law and her husband's other relatives. If a woman is content in her husband's homestead, she will probably tolerate or ignore her husband's amorous adventures.

We cannot overstress the point that the relationship of a woman to her mother-in-law is central to the stability of a Limbu marriage. In Limbu society, unlike our society, the man remains distant from his in-laws while the woman, as a result of residence after marriage, not only comes into direct daily contact with her in-laws but frequently, in the early years, the mother-in-law lives in the same house. There she exercises an oppressive and ubiquitous role as watchdog. She tests the young bride daily, both in her skill at household chores and in her fidelity to her son, and if the girl fails in her duties, slows down in her work, or begins to wander in the weekly bazaars and flirt with other men, she is chastised severely. It is no wonder that those who run off with other men in "adulterous marriage" most frequently cite as their reasons the inability to endure the mother-in-law. As one girl said, "It is impossible to please the mother-in-law. She is never satisfied."

Adulterous liaisons almost always occur in the early stages of a woman's first marriage, before she has taken up residence in her husband's homestead. Over 80 percent of the twenty-one "adulterous marriages" recorded in 1968–69 involved women who had been married less than three years to their first husband.

Table 1
Frequency of Divorce in Relation
to the Completion of Marriage Payments
(Compiled from Genealogies)

| Completion of marriage payments | Number of marriage separations | Percent of total |
|---|---|---|
| Prior to 1st annual payment | 12 | 50.00 |
| Prior to 2nd annual payment | 6 | 25.00 |
| Prior to final annual payment | 2 | 8.33 |
| After completion of all payments | 2 | 8.33 |
| Unknown | 2 | 8.34 |
| | 24 | 100.00% |

All twenty-one women were either living in their natal homes or had returned there for extended visits after conflicts with their in-laws. The low incidence of "adulterous marriages" after the first three years of marriage is attributable to the birth of children and the completion of the marriage payments.

## Children Are Marriage Stabilizers

The birth of children usually stabilizes a precarious marriage. Only one of the twenty-four recorded separations in 1968–69 involved a marriage where the woman was a mother. A young childless woman living in her husband's household is the object of furious resentment by the other women. She is treated somewhat as a servant or a child until she has given birth to children, when she becomes an equal.

Most Limbu wives for this reason will not move into the conjugal home until they have given birth to their first child, which often happens during the first three years of marriage. A case in many ways typical was that of a girl living near us who moved to her husband's household when she had a baby boy, two years after marriage. Prior to the birth, she refused to live in her husband's household because the work was too hard and her mother-in-law always screamed at her. After the birth she felt certain her mother-in-law would abate her criticism. Apparently the girl's expectations were not entirely fulfilled, however.

When Rex returned in 1975, he found her living part of the year with her husband and part of the year in her natal home. During his stay she was at her natal home, and her son was now seven years old. In addition, she had given birth to a baby girl, then two years old. When asked why she was not living with her husband, she laughed and said, "It's easier here; my mother-in-law demands a lot of work. My husband is nice, but it's nicer to be home." Thus even after nine years of apparently successful marriage, this woman still had not fully committed herself to life with her in-laws.

In Case History 6 (chapter 5), the wife remained in her natal home for five years after marriage until she finally bore a child. Today she lives peacefully with her husband although in 1968–69 she argued frequently with her mother-in-law.

The birth of a boy stabilizes a marriage more solidly than the birth of a girl does. The Limbu desire sons as heirs since a daughter will eventually marry and move away and will not stay to care for the family estate. One woman who had given birth to a daughter before moving in with her husband often told us in 1968–69 that if she had borne a boy, things would have been better for her. By 1975, this woman's wish had been fulfilled—indeed, she then had two boys and two girls. Her expectations concerning her mother-in-law's attitude also proved correct, as she and the older woman now lived happily under the same roof. The mother-in-law no longer complained, and even boasted of her daughter-in-law's accomplishments.

Thus, as we have seen, a young wife's problems usually revolve around her mother-in-law, whose presence makes most new Limbu marriages potentially explosive. And thus the young wife often returns to her natal home to live as in the above cases, until she has given birth. During this period at home she is relatively free to rid herself of an undesirable mate by running away with another man.

## Polygynous Marriage

Occasionally a husband takes a second wife, which may trigger violence and, ultimately, divorce. Most of the polygynous marriages in the 1968–69 sample (14 out of 17) were contracted after the first wife failed to produce children, especially sons. The Limbu, who themselves laugh at a man who has two or more wives, nonetheless acknowledge that barrenness is a valid reason for taking a second wife. Any other excuse, however, is regarded as frivolous and fair game for gossip.

One co-wife usually remains in her natal homestead, or sometimes a husband builds a separate household for a co-wife on his *kipat* land, and divides one household into two. The inability of his wives to get along harmoniously is the reason given, but if *kipat* land is separated by long distances, it helps to have the family living close to the divided property. In an actual case, a retired Gurkha officer had two wives living in separate expensive households on divided land. Because he was extremely wealthy and commanded a large annual pension as a retired soldier, he could afford the extra costs.

Polygynous marriages are frequently taken as grounds for divorce or for one wife to run away with another man. These separations almost invariably result from the inability of the two wives to coexist, a situation which (as noted above) is alleviated by having the wives live apart. In Case History 22 in chapter 5, the husband took a second wife, and the first wife, who had never moved permanently into her husband's household, sought a legal divorce at the instigation of her father. Other unstable marriages could be attributed to squabbles between co-wives (see Case Histories 3, 4, 8, 12, 16, and 21).

126

Monogamous unions are generally much more stable than polygynous marriages. One two-wife household that we were familiar with was filled with the husband's anxieties and frustrations. The wives were always quarrelling, and the man spent hours pacifying grievances and mediating disputes (see Case History 3). In households where co-wives live under the same roof, fights are everyday occurrences and sometimes include physical combat. We knew of instances where Nepali bushknives came into play, and in one case a co-wife was beaten so badly she had to flee for her very life.

Instability during the trial period of a polygynous marriage is counteracted by gift exchange, the birth of children, and the ability of the bride to trace kinship ties to other in-marrying women in the husband's homestead and patrilineage.

## Exchange Marriages

A woman's discontent with in-laws is tempered when two or more sisters of one clan marry two or more brothers of another clan. In such instances, a person who shares a kinship relation to a clansman's wife is sought. The Limbu also feel that brother and sister exchange marriage is ideal, when a brother of one clan gives a clan "sister" to the man of another clan, in exchange for a sister of that man's clan. Table 2 shows the frequency of such marriages.

*Table 2*
Frequency of Marriages Involving "Brother" and "Sister"
(Compiled from Genealogies)

| Type of marriage | Number of marriages | Percentage |
|---|---|---|
| Actual or fictive sisters married to actual or fictive brothers | 34 | 21.8 |
| Brother/sister exchange marriages | 6 | 3.8 |
| Other | 116 | 74.4 |
| | 156 | 100.0% |

Not a single separation involving brother/sister exchange marriages was recorded, which indicates their stability compared to marriages in which kinship relations were remote or untraceable. Case History 20 in

127

chapter 5 depicts the nature of these marriages, and in Case History 5, an "adulterous marriage," the girl left her first husband to marry a man whose brother was married to her elder sister. This example describes the woman's desire for a more compatible conjugal situation through "adultery marriage" and also the strength of a marriage when a woman can trace kinship ties to other residents of her husband's village.

If sisters are unable to marry brothers, they will try to trace kinship ties in other generations. A girl will endeavor to marry into a household or village where she has patrilineal kinswomen. The most successful marriages in Limbuan involve a wife who has kinswomen married to her husband's close kinsmen. The Limbu approve these marriages and stress the importance of kinship ties in all arranged marriages to insure success.

## The Woman Is Vital to Marriage Stability

The woman, rather than the man, is the deciding factor in Limbu marriage stability. Her marriage expectations must be at least minimally fulfilled if a successful relationship is to be maintained. The husband's expectations are to a great extent fulfilled at the time of the wedding ceremony. Prior to that time he has complete freedom in selecting a spouse, and after that time his life is basically unaltered. Relatives and lifelong friends comprise his household. If his wife is sexually incompatible or if she fails to produce children, he can by tradition take another wife without dissolving his first marriage. The woman, on the other hand, has but two avenues open to her if her hopes are thwarted—she can return to her natal home or she can run away to live with another man. The relief afforded her by the first route is usually temporary, for eventually her parents will pressure her either to stay married (since they are the beneficiaries of her marriage contract through bridewealth) or to seek another husband.

The uncomfortable and often traumatic dilemma of the Limbu wife is further complicated because the Limbu are inclined to arrange marriages over great distances. It is extremely difficult for a woman far from home to be reinforced by her natal kinsmen if her marital situation is frustrating and worrisome. She may find herself among strangers who are completely indifferent to her emotional needs. Thus she is faced with people who share patrilineal kinship, yet are potentially hostile to in-marrying females who might threaten their daily routine or prove to be lazy.

128

Geographical distance from one's natal home may be compounded by linguistic differences; the Limbu speak at least four mutually unintelligible dialects (Mewa Khola, Maiwa Khola, Phedap, and Panchthar). A woman who speaks a different dialect from that of her husband's household may have problems expressing herself to her in-laws as well as understanding them, and such problems can only make her feel more alienated.

The likelihood that a Limbu woman will marry into a strange regional and linguistic background is much higher than for the neighboring Rai or other ethnic groups, who tend to marry within the same village or into a neighboring village. We feel that the reasons for this difference are intimately related to the freedom which the Limbu men and women enjoy in choosing spouses through their peculiar patterns of courtship. The rice dance, in particular, enables them to meet potential spouses from all over Limbuan.

Once a stable marriage has been established between partners separated by distance and language, the plight of subsequent newcomers can be eased if they follow the ideal marriage pattern of sisters marrying brothers. This pattern fosters the growth of comfortable affinal relationships on all sides, and the wedding ceremonies that bring about such unions provide an opportunity for Limbu boys and girls who share this relationship to meet and dance. For those women who will not or cannot establish tolerable lives for themselves in their husbands' homes, however, marital instability is inevitable.

# The Limbu Woman
## and the Position of Women in South Asia

## 7

*"Gone are the days of the vigorous feminism and anti-feminism. The way is now cleared for a consideration of how a woman's position in society varies, if it does, with types of culture and social structure without having to take up the cudgels on behalf of anybody or anything."*

—Evans-Pritchard (1963:40)

The central message in the statement quoted above has become muddied in the tide of women's liberation issues raised in the last decade. Indeed it seems that in our familiar world a great many people, feminists and anti-feminists alike, are taking up cudgels on behalf of many things. Much of their debate turns on the fundamental, inherent differences between "male" and "female," as if settling that question would settle once and for all the question of woman's just and proper role the world over.

Our purpose in writing this book was not to enter this debate, but rather to attend to the more modest and less impassioned task suggested by Evans-Pritchard. We have intended simply to present an ethnographic description of the social role of Limbu women as we came to understand it during our field research, and ultimately perhaps to shed some new light on the *diversity* of female roles in south Asia and elsewhere.

Although our primary intent was to depict the Limbu woman in marriage, divorce, and the family, we have not overlooked the role of the Limbu man. That would have been impossible, for as the reader by now must surely see, the lives of Limbu men and women—like the lives of men and women everywhere—are inextricably interwoven. Any attempt to impose an artificial separation would have resulted in a flawed image of the people who so generously gave us their hospitality and the opportunity to carry out our research. Our book thus of necessity describes not so much how Limbu women live as individuals, as how women and men live together in Limbu society.

The projected "ideal" for married women in mainstream American culture has long suggested to us that women should stay home, take care of the house, and raise children. Mother should be well-groomed, not necessarily too bright, and somewhat helpless. Projected on television and radio, and in children's stories and women's magazines, is the concept the authors themselves grew up with: "Men bring home the bacon; women cook it." Many Americans still believe that the division of labor and characterization of the way women are "supposed to be" is inevitable, or even ordained. The current backlash to the women's liberation movement bears this out. Only weeks before the final manuscript of *The Himalayan Woman* was completed, the Equal Rights Amendment, designed to give equality to women in public activities, was soundly defeated in the State of New York. Not long afterward, there appeared a popular book called *The Total Woman*, which chastised the feminist movement and urged women "back to the kitchen." Limbu men and women would undoubtedly find Americans' attitudes puzzling, if not laughable. Women in Limbuan are actively encouraged to enter the marketplace, and the Limbu men of today would never demand that a woman confine herself solely to the kitchen and domestic activities.

The relative status of men and women in most societies is comparable only within a group, whether a class, a caste, a community or a family. In the Judeo-Christian countries, where until recently, most anthropologists were reared, male domination over females is often taken for granted. Limbu women, on the other hand, have always been respected as individuals and as workers, and especially as child-bearers. In the institution of marriage, if a bride is purchased, there is the explicit and implicit recognition that what is purchased is not the body of the woman but the right to her work potential and the children she will bear. In the life-cycle rituals women are equated with life-giving forces and men with the forces of death. The seclusion of women in childbirth and menstruation and the refusal of men to eat food cooked by menstruating women should not be taken as a sign that female biological processes are thought to be dirty, evil, or somehow degrading. On the contrary, these processes, held in high esteem by both men and women, are recognized as the most powerful forces in nature and the perpetuation of life itself.

Anthropologists studying societies in which marriage functions as a system of alliance to unite families, have often viewed marriage as a weapon in the political battlefield and women as pawns in the political games men play. Very early on, our field experience in Limbuan appeared to belie this passive conception of the woman's role in marriage. We therefore tried to frame our research questions to elicit subjective perspectives that would reveal women as active strategists who are able to make and affect decisions about their own lives. We have viewed marriage as a process rather than an act and have examined this process in terms of the everyday decisions that individual Limbu must make in order to undertake, maintain, or dissolve a marriage.

Contracting marriages depends largely on the decisions men make keeping in mind the possible formation of alliances over all Limbuan. However, the maintenance and dissolution of a marriage relationship is vitally affected by the role of women in marriage and family life. It is, after all, usually the woman who must adjust to living and working with the group of strangers in her husband's household. If she cannot make this adjustment, she invariably ends the marriage by leaving her husband, and usually by running off with another man.


## Women in South Asia

The Limbu woman's part in marriage and family life is not unique to peoples living in south Asia, even high-caste Hindus in parts of India. Berreman (1963:168), in a study of peoples in the Himalayas of Uttar Pradesh in India west of Nepal, notes that divorce rates there are around 20 percent in all castes, and that women are responsible for most of the breakups in marriage. In a study of a village in central India, Mayer (1960:234–235) notes that a woman divorces a man by running away with another, and that this act, or its threat, lessens the power and authority of men.

Pauline Kolenda (1966) has written a very important paper in which she compares family types in six different parts of India, and attributes the diversity of the Indian family to the key part women play in marriage. She made the claim that a low divorce rate seems to be characteristic of areas with a large number of Hindu joint family households, and that a high divorce rate seems to correlate with the occurrence of the nuclear family household in India. She attributes high divorce rates to the strong ties that women have with their natal families, especially to the ties that men have to their wives' families. When a woman has close natal ties and a man recognizes these ties through long-term economic or social obligations to her family (as in extended bridewealth payments or labor services), the divorce rate is likely to be higher and the joint-family household absent. Nickolas' (1966) data from west Bengal supports Kolenda's hypothesis.

The Limbu family and marriage fit this general pattern, and an understanding of the Limbu woman's active role in society is crucial to an understanding of Limbu family life. In Limbuan nuclear family households predominate, the bridewealth payments are extensive and drawn out, and the Limbu have a relatively high rate of marriage instability and divorce.

In a more recent volume, Goody and Tambiah (1973) have suggested that in societies in which bridewealth is paid there is an associated tendency toward female independence in economic and social roles and a strong general tendency toward egalitarian relations between the sexes. By contrast, in those societies which adhere to the dowry tradition, women are more economically restricted and are expected to be passive in social and sexual relations with men. The latter societies also show a marked tendency toward social stratification. Again, our Limbu information supports these generalizations, since Limbu society is characterized by high bridewealth payments and relative egalitarianism, and its women are relatively independent economically, socially, and sexually.

Marriage and the family in south Asia viewed from the woman's perspective is changing our western conceptions and stereotypes of the traditional Indian family. It is no longer possible to think of the typical south Asian family as an extended family in which the women are secluded and confined to the role of domestics and childbearers. These are not the only activities in which women participate, nor are they alike from one village to another or from one caste or ethnic group to another.

Consequently, the woman in south Asia is not typically a passive, shy, and secluded creature, but more often an active participant in the economy and social life of the village. In many regions, the woman has a culturally recognized right to make significant and far-reaching decisions about her own life, decisions which may have repercussions in many other areas of the society. We are not saying that Limbu women, or any women in south Asia, have achieved an ideal state of equality with men and a total independence in public activities. But their independence has frequently been overlooked and misunderstood. We hope that this book will have an impact on future research in the area, and on the already changing view of the role of women in marriage and the family.

## Limbu Women's Lives: A Final Look

In Limbuan, people must work hard to feed themselves. Brothers and sisters, husbands and wives, grandmothers and grandsons must work together to eke out an existence on the available land. Limbu women have strong backs and arms; they can carry heavy loads, chop wood, and join in the arduous tasks of planting, cultivating and harvesting.

During the busy agricultural season from April to November, all adults work in the fields while the young children keep an eye on each other or on their family cows, chickens, goats, and pigs. During the off-season, women spend busy days collecting and storing wood, weaving cloth, and processing grains. Some men take advantage of their leisure time to carry out trading ventures or travel in the hills or lowlands to buy and sell goods for extra cash. Others perform seasonal agricultural work in India, or conduct the political affairs of Limbuan.

Whatever the time of year, the Limbu woman's day begins before sunrise. One woman from each household sets a large clay jug in an enormous basket, squats in front of the basket and arranges a tumpline across her forehead, hoists the basket and jug onto her head, and goes to fetch the day's supply of water. When young married women living with their husbands perform this task, they often leave the children sleeping with their fathers. Older women send their teenage daughters to get water or, better yet, a young daughter-in-law who resides in the house.

Houses stir as the inhabitants prepare for their daily work or pleasure. There is much hacking and coughing and throat clearing, much splashing of water on sleepy faces—all part of the morning's small rituals of cleanliness. Women returning from the water fountains put down their burdens and join the others as they go out to their chores, which vary as the seasons change.

Young children are often left in the care of older siblings. A nursing mother returning from the fields might pause long enough to give a two-year-old a quick "snack" before she cooks the rice. Babies accompany their mothers on the round of tasks, wrapped close to the mothers' bodies by cotton shawls which serve as combination raincoats-hats-

134

baby-buggies-knapsacks and—slung halfway across faces—veil-like protectors of female modesty.

Late in the morning, one woman from the house returns to cook the first rice meal of the day, which might take an hour or more to prepare. Rice or corn mush, a vegetable or a lentil dish or two—each must be cooked in turn on the one available fire. Men of the household are served first, followed perhaps by a senior wife, mother, or mother-in-law, older sons, daughters, young children, and lastly the young wife, who finishes everyone else's leftovers. After the meal is eaten, the family members return to their tasks. The cook or her younger sisters or daughters wash the pots and plates and return to their other chores.

In winter the women may spend hours in the sun, spinning thread or picking lice out of their own or their children's hair. A trip to the forest to collect wood is made less tedious when a large group goes, so young girls accompany their mothers and sisters, carrying small baskets to fill with wood. Women of several households cooperate in setting up the elaborate machinery used to press oil, and work then becomes a social occasion. When a woman distills liquor, which takes several hours, neighboring women gather to taste the product and offer a sometimes brutally honest judgment on its quality.

Sometime during the afternoon, one of the wives prepares a snack of beer, popped corn, roasted soybeans, or roasted or boiled corn or potatoes. In the busy agricultural season, when help outside the family or localized lineage members is needed to complete a project, the women of the house will bring a sumptuous snack to the fields for the family to share.

After the day's work is done in the fields, the women return home to cook a second meal of rice, prepared inside the small dark houses lit only by the cooking fire. In the winter, the smoky houses keep everyone warm; in the summer, the smoke helps keep mosquitoes away. When the meal is finished, the dishes are scraped and washed with cold water and ashes. Young people can be found with their friends in a dance or at a ritual in the house in the evenings, while the older Limbu women converse and drink liquor until they drift off to sleep.

On market days, the routine is interrupted. Rice is cooked early so the women can start selling their wares or buying whatever items are to be purchased early in the morning. Young girls dress in their finery, hoping to meet young men friends and arrange a dance for the evening. Limbu women living near the bazaars open their houses to friends and relatives who stop to talk, visit, and sell or purchase beer or liquor.

Late-afternoon visitors to our house on market day had a special glow that came from the liberal consumption of strong liquor. One visitor stands out in our memories—a Limbu woman in her forties. She squatted on the floor in our kitchen and showed us the garlic, ginger, and vegetables she had purchased at the market that day. We all had a little to drink, and we half laughed and half cried as she brought each item into view, then carefully divided the lot into two piles. "One for Kanchi (as Shirley was known in the hills), one for me. One for Kanchi, one for me." Several months later, the woman was dead, and we attended her funeral.

Weddings, special holidays, and festivals are occasions during which the everyday life of the Limbu woman comes to a halt. The most extreme example occurs when the bride's friends accompany her to the wedding and have a three- or four-day holiday, are waited upon and do little or no work. Young women spend the whole night dancing and celebrating.

Women often travel half a day or more, with no male escorts, to attend such festivities, or to visit their natal home. They go in pairs or in groups of three or four, sometimes with babies on their backs. They wear their finest clothes and borrow gold necklaces and earrings for adornment.

Ambitious women may combine pleasure with business enterprise. One young woman we knew, unmarried at the age of twenty-two, invited us to go with her to a three-day festival, half a day's walk away. In advance of the appointed day, she borrowed fifteen rupees from us to buy a quantity of unhusked rice and spent two days flattening the rice into a Nepali snack. She and her younger sister carried the food with them to the festival, where they spent the days selling and the nights dancing.

Despite the many occasions when Limbu women leave their homes either for work or pleasure, having and raising children is a central part of their lives. Childbirth seems to be relatively painless (we heard stories of babies being born in the fields while the pregnant women squatted to defecate), and at the birth of a child the mother is treated like a queen. She is called by a special name, given presents of rice and oil, chickens and herbs, and friends come to visit. Often a woman will return to her natal home before the baby is due to spend the time after childbirth in privacy and leisure with no mother-in-law around.

Limbu women are playful with their children. They will tease a young boy about his "peanut," and grab at his genitals. Children are rarely disciplined or treated harshly. A baby who urinates or defecates

136

## The Death of a Limbu Woman

*Above:* Family and lineage members surround a dead Limbu woman before the funeral. *Right:* Limbu women sit on a hill overlooking the cemetery while the men dig the grave.

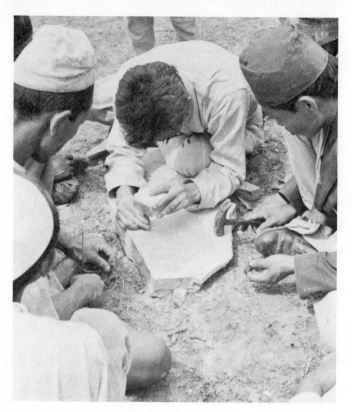

*Above:* A man engraves the grave-stone. *Below:* Men make delicate paper flowers to be used in the *bharki. Above right:* Huge pots of rice are cooked to feed the guests at *bharki. Below right:* Family members gather to give a final feast to the spirit of the deceased.

138

on the mother's lap will simply be lifted up, and a dog called over to clean up the mess.

It is not uncommon for a Limbu woman to see over half the children she has produced die before they reach five years of age. Those children who die are believed to have been taken away by the angry spirits of other dead children. They, in turn, become evil spirits against whom future children of their mothers or close female relatives must be protected. A woman whose child is sick must ask the help of a Limbu shaman to capture the spirit of her dead child and keep its ghost from attacking her living children. One woman who described this process to us indicated poignantly the depth of her enduring love for her dead child. When her baby had died and became an angry spirit, he had tried to eat other children and caused her to have a miscarriage. Now her second baby, a girl, was sickly. Clearly the dead child's spirit would have to be captured, but still the mother hesitated because she "loved the dead child" and did not want to disturb its spirit. Finally she consented, the ceremony was performed, and her girl child lived.

The death of an older child may also cause a mother deep grief. One day at a nearby household, our neighbors told us that a woman had come to visit from her home, several days' walk away. Since her teen-aged son had died, the woman had been so grief-stricken she was unable to stay in her own home. She spent several months visiting her relatives to console herself.

Limbu women worry fiercely when their children are sick and often sell gold to pay for the healing ceremonies that are deemed necessary. The fears that assail them at such times are likely to go well beyond the normal universal ones. One night, our cook, whose husband had been gone in Assam for six years, told us that she was unhappy because her son was sick and she had a frightening dream the night before. She dreamt she had seen a man sleeping in a house. One wall and the roof were separated from the rest of the house where her family and children were gathered. This she took to be an omen that her house would die. In the months that followed, she was repeatedly possessed by a Limbu diety, Yuma Summang (see S. Jones 1976). She, as well as neighboring Limbu, became convinced that she soon would apprentice to a Limbu shaman and become a Yuma, or female shaman.

Six months after we came to Tehrathum, our cook's husband returned to Limbuan, intending to take her back with him to a new home in Assam. She and her children had been living on her husband's land and moreover had grown accustomed to the higher standard of living we provided. When her husband returned, she hesitated at first to leave.

Going to Assam with him would mean leaving behind the life and friends she had known for the last fifteen years, plus six additional months of salary and benefits she would earn by working for us.

Her husband waited while she remained indecisive for over a month. Finally, she decided to go to Assam with her husband and children. Once the decision was made, she left Limbuan loaded down with the family possessions on her back, following behind her husband who led the way unburdened except for his walking-stick to give him direction.

## The Role of the Limbu Woman: A Summary

Limbu women are mothers, yet child-rearing is shared by husbands, older children, sisters, brothers, sisters-in-law, brothers-in-law, grandmothers, and grandfathers. Women keep house, usually a limited responsibility because of the paucity of material possessions. Women are responsible for meals, although older daughters and other relatives may do most of the actual cooking. In addition, they are largely responsible for food production, for a variety of necessary crafts, and for selling their wares in the marketplace.

Older women's opinions are respected; they help make decisions regarding the use and disposition of family land and act as ritual household heads if their male peers are dead or absent. Women do whatever tasks they can well into old age and remain productive members of the household until they die.

A Limbu woman may decide if she will marry and whom she will marry. Frequently she is allowed, even encouraged, to exert her independence in marriage. She can find happiness both as a productive member of society and as a wife and mother. Finally, if a Limbu woman enters into a household filled with loneliness and conflict, she can resolve her problem by ending the marriage.

The Limbu woman's position in society seems to be directly related to her active participation in the Limbu economy. Her status is not solely determined by her position as a domestic or childbearer; she brings cash into the household and shares in the work of agricultural production. In many ways she is able to acquire an equality with men in the "extra-domestic" or "public" sphere of Limbu social relations despite the patriarchal nature of Limbu marital, domestic, and public institutions.

The Limbu woman's productive capacity does not seem to be greatly affected by her role as childbearer and childrearer. She lives within cooperative groups and extended families, and there are always other women, older siblings and children, or sometimes men, available to look after young children. Perhaps because of the hardships of mountain life and the difficulties in transportation and communication, her physical mobility is somewhat circumscribed compared to a man's: she neither actively engages in migrant labor nor enters into military service. But her contributions to household budgets and to the Limbu economy are now of equal importance to a man's, and by successfully combining domestic and extradomestic activities she has moved steadily closer to full-scale equality.

The actual division of labor between Limbu men and women is recognized by the people themselves as extremely flexible. Women are never "put down" by Limbu men because of their childbearing role and their domestic labor; on the contrary, the men respect them the more for their contributions in these spheres. Finally, Limbu women are certainly not thought to be "weak" and "passive" when compared to men. More than once we heard Limbu men praise the women for their strength, endurance, and ability to work long hard hours, almost as if to say that a man, who frequently fritters away his time talking and traveling from house-to-house instead of doing business, is in truth weaker.

# Glossary of Native Terms

All of the native terms listed below were originally Nepali (Indo-Aryan) words which have been adopted by the bilingual Limbu and are commonly used by them even when they are speaking their native Tibeto-Burman language.

bharki
: a Limbu mourning ritual or wake

chori bihā
: marriage by theft or elopement; marriage without brideprice

dhān nāch
: "rice dance" or Limbu courtship dance

dharma
: religion; way of life; social and moral duty and obligation

dukha
: hurt; misery; suffering

jāri bihā
: adulterous marriage; runaway marriage; marriage to a woman who is already married, followed by divorce and compensation

jutho
: pollution; impurity; usually refers to food taboos, especially at funerals, wakes, or the acceptance of cooked food and water between members of different social groups and castes

kanchi
: youngest sister or daughter

karma
: fate; one's supernatural power that determines position in society

| | |
|---|---|
| *kipat* | the communal land tenure system in east Nepal; land owned and controlled by an ethnic group, in this case the Limbu |
| *māgi bihā* | marriage by arrangement, usually arranged by the families of the bride and groom |
| *paysa (pice)* | a coin; Nepali "cents"; the rupee consists of 100 paysa or "cents" |
| *raikar* | freehold land tenure system; ownership is individual regardless of ethnic group affiliation |
| *rupee* | Nepali money; the *rupee* consists of 100 *paysa*; at time of the author's first visit to Nepal the exchange rate was approximately 10 rupees to the dollar |
| *saimundri* | final Limbu marriage payment from husband to wife's family; signifies the transfer of the wife's name and social obligations to that of the husband's family |
| *sukha* | happiness; good health |
| *tikā* | a blessing; frequently refers to a mixture of rice and curd applied to the forehead on ceremonial occasions; also refers to a mark on the forehead for adornment |

# Glossary of Anthropological Terms

brideprice
the initial payment in marriage from the husband and his family to the bride's family. Considered to be a payment for the services of the bride, the right to legitimize her children, and compensation to her parents for the loss of a daughter

bridewealth
the sum total of all payments made to the bride's family by the husband and his family in a lifetime

clan
a named group of people who trace their descent and kinship to a common ancestor; a unilineal descent group with exogamous marriage

descent
kinship affiliation determined by tracing ties to a lineal ancestor

extended family
a family that includes two or more nuclear families with common residence and related by descent

junior levirate
the process by which a woman marries her dead husband's younger brother

junior sororate
the process by which a man marries his dead wife's younger sister

145

| | |
|---|---|
| *lineage* | a group of people (not necessarily named or exogamous) tracing unilineal descent to a common ancestor; a kinship segment of a clan |
| *marriage* | the contractual union of a man and woman that is recognized as legal and produces legitimate offspring |
| *marriage stability* | the degree to which a married couple maintains stable conjugal relations free from long-term separations or divorce |
| *nuclear family* | a family consisting of husband and wife and their unmarried children, occasionally including a widowed parent or other unattached kinsman |
| *patrilineal descent* | a descent relationship traced exclusively through male ancestors |
| *patrilocal residence* | the process by which husband and wife take up residence in the husband's father's household after marriage |
| *polygyny* | the marriage of a man to two or more women at the same time |

# Bibliography

Berreman, Gerald
　1963　*Hindus of the Himalayas.* Berkeley: University of California Press.

Caplan, L.
　1966　"Land and Social Change in East Nepal." Ph.D. Dissertation. Anthropology Department, School of Oriental and African Studies, University of London.

　1967　Some Political Consequences of State Land Policy in East Nepal. *Man* 2:107–14.

　1970　*Land and Social Change in East Nepal: A Study of Hindu-Tribal Relations.* Berkeley and Los Angeles: Univ. of California Press.

　1974　A Himalayan People: Limbus of Nepal. In *South Asia: Seven Community Profiles,* Clarence Maloney, ed., pp. 173–201, New York: Holt, Rinehart and Winston.

Chemjong, Iman Sing
　1967　*History and Culture of the Kirat People,* Parts I and II. Kathmandu: Private Publication.

Cohen, Ronald
　1961　Marriage Instability among the Kanuri of Northern Nigeria. *American Anthropologist* 63:1231–48.

Evans-Pritchard, E. E.
    1934    Social Character of Bride-Wealth, with Special Reference to the Azande. *Man* 194:172–75.

    1951    *Kinship and Marriage among the Nuer.* Oxford: Clarendon Press.

    1963    *On the Position of Women in Society and Other Essays.* London: Faber and Faber.

Fallers, Lloyd
    1957    Some Determinants of Marriage Stability in Busoga: A Reformulation of Gluckman's Thesis. *Africa* 27:106–21.

Fürer-Haimendorf, C. von
    1964    *The Sherpas of Nepal: Buddhist Highlanders.* Calcutta: Oxford Book Company.

Gluckman, Max
    1950    Kinship and Marriage among the Lozi of Northern Rhodesia and the Zulu of Natal. In *African Systems of Kinship and Marriage*, A. R. Radcliffe-Brown and Daryll Forde, eds. pp. 166–206. London: Oxford University Press.

Goody, Jack and S. J. Tambiah, eds.
    1973    *Bridewealth and Dowry.* Cambridge: Cambridge University Press.

Goody, Jack
    1962    Conjugal Separation and Divorce among the Gonja of Northern Ghana. In *Marriage in Tribal Societies.* Cambridge: Cambridge University Press.

Hitchcock, John T.
    1966    *The Magars of Banyan Hill.* New York: Holt, Rinehart and Winston.

Jones, Rex L.
    1973    "Kinship and Marriage among the Limbu of Eastern Nepal: a Study in Marriage Stability." Ph.D. Dissertation. Ann Arbor: University Microfilms.

    1974    Religious Symbolism in Limbu Death by Violence. *Omega* 5(3):252–66.

    1976a   Sanskritization in Eastern Nepal. *Ethnology* 15(1):63–76.

    1976b   Limbu Spirit Possession and Shamanism. In *Spirit Possession in the Nepal Himalaya*, John T. Hitchcock and Rex L. Jones, eds., pp. 29–55. Warminster: Aris and Phillips, Ltd.

Jones, Shirley Kurz
    1976    Limbu Spirit Possession: A Case Study. In *Spirit Possession in the Nepal Himalaya*, John T. Hitchcock and Rex L. Jones, eds., pp. 22–28. Warminster: Aris and Phillips, Ltd.

*148*

Kolenda, Pauline
    1966   Regional Differences in Indian Family Structure. In *Regions and Regionalism in South Asian Studies: an Exploratory Study*, Robert I. Crane, ed., pp. 147–226, 1967, Duke University: Monographs and Occasional Papers, Series No. 5.

Leach, Edmund
    1957   Aspects of Bridewealth and Marriage Stability among the Kachin and Lakher. *Man* 57:50–55.

Lewis, I.M.
    1962   *Marriage and the Family in Northern Somaliland.* Kampala: East African Institute of Research.

Lloyd, Peter C.
    1968   Divorce among the Yoruba. *American Anthropologist* 70:68–81.

Mayer, Adrian
    1960   *Caste and Kinship in Central India: A Village and Its Region.* Berkeley and Los Angeles: University of California Press.

Nickolas, Ralph
    1966   Comment on the Paper by Pauline Kolenda. In *Regions and Regionalism in South Asian Studies: an Exploratory Study*, Robert I. Crane, ed., pp. 227–231, 1967, Duke University: Monographs and Occasional Papers, Series No. 5.

Pignède, Bernard
    1966   *Les Gurung, une population himalayenne du Nepal.* Paris: Mouton.

Regmi, Makesh C.
    1965   *Land Tenure and Taxation in Nepal: The Jagir, Rakam, and Kipat Systems.* Berkeley: Institute of International Studies, vol. III, Research Series No. 8.

Rosser, Colin
    1966   Social Mobility in the Newar Caste System. In *Caste and Kin in Nepal, India, and Ceylon: Anthropological Studies in Hindu-Buddhist Contact Zones*, C. von Fürer-Haimendorf, ed., pp. 68–139. Bombay: Asia Publishing House.

Sagant, Philippe
    1969a Les marches en pays Limbu: Notes sur trois *hat bajar* des districts de Taplejung et de Tehrathum. *L'Ethnographie*, pp. 90–118.

    1969b Mariage par enlèvement chez les Limbu (Nepal). *Cahiers Internationaux de Sociologie* 48:71–98.

Schneider, David M.
    1953   A Note on Bridewealth and the Stability of Marriage. *Man* 53:55–57.

Turner, Victor W.

1957 *Schism and Continuity in an African Society.* Manchester: Manchester University Press.

# Index

*152*

India: images of, 33–34; women in, 131–34

Inheritance, patterns of, 49–53; by women, 69–70

In-laws: and marriage stability, 102–3, 105, 106–8, 110, 114, 115, 119, 120, 122, 123–24, 125–26

Intermediator, role of in arranging marriages, 59–60, 62–63, 80–82, 92

Jaisi Brahman, 39

*Jāri Bihā. See* Marriage "by adultery"

Junior levirate, 67–68

Junior sororate, 68, 115–16

Kathmandu, 12

Kinship: as focus of anthropological study, 3–4; and forms of personal address, 121; importance of, in settling marriage disputes, 106–7; and marriage stability, 5, 117–18, 127–28, 129; and weekly markets, 18–19. *See also* Clans; Lineage

*Kipat,* 35–36, 38, 41, 45–46, 47, 50–51, 55, 126

Kirati, 8

Kontsokma Sammang, 94

Lahorang Rai, 8

Land ownership: and family inheritance patterns, 51–53; patterns of, in Limbuan, 35; as source of political conflict between Limbu and Hindu, 34–37, 45. *See also Kipat; Raikar*

Language: as source of marriage instability, 128–29; and forms of personal address within family, 121; and Limbu social structure and culture, 41–42

Lending, as Limbu custom, 31–32

Life cycle, rituals at major events of, 93–99

Limbu: caste among, 39–41; clothing of, 42–43; dietary customs of, 44–45; economic dependence on Hindus of, 35–37; land ownership by, 35–37; language variations among, 41–42; nationalism of, 45–46, 48; religious practices of, 43

Limbuan: culture of, compared to Hindu, 41–45; effect of Hindus on social customs, 46–48; ethnic groups of, 10–11; history, climate, geography of, 8–11; land ownership in, 34–37; sources of income in, 37–39

Lineage: as component of clans, 54–55; and marriage gifts, 62–63; as political force, 55–56; and ritual pollution, 53–54

Liquor, 21–22; as marriage gift, 62–64, 66; production of, 135; as income source, 38. *See also* Alcohol; Beer

Macdougal, Charles, 2

Magar, 2, 10–11, 16, 39, 65

Maiwa Khola, 8, 128

Market economy: effect on women's role in family, 70–71; penetration of Limbuan by, 35–37, 46–47

Markets. *See* Weekly markets

Marriage: defined, 4; effect of social upheaval in Limbuan on, 47–48; factors affecting stability of, 120–29; as focus of anthropological study, 3–5; ideal of, in United States, 131; in early 19th-century Limbuan, 47; Limbu and Hindu, compared, 43–44, 132–34 *passim*

Marriage "by adultery" *(Jari biha),* 66–67, 76–77, 104–5, 109, 122–24, 127; and compensation to injured spouse, 105–6 111, 112, 113–14, 115, 118, 119; as expression of male dominance, 69; and "loose" women, 110–11, 114–15; and male promiscuity, 114–15

Marriage "by arrangement": age of partners at first, 80; compared to other cultures in South Asia, 132–34; and exchange of gifts, 58–64, 110; and geographical distance from bride's natal household, 128–29; place of childless wife in, 120, 125; and reluctance of bride to move into husband's household, 107, 110, 125–26; with members of different ethnic and caste groups, 65–66

Marriage "by theft" *(Chori biha),* 66, 76–77, 109; as expression of male dominance, 69

Meat: dietary habits regarding, 16–17; as marriage gift, 62–63, 66

Men: customary authority of, 69; status of, in rituals, 99–100, 131–32; work assigned to, 25–31, 141–42

Menstruation, 131–32; and ritual pollution, 93, 98–99, 100

Mewa Khola, 8, 128

Midwife, 96–97, 98

Mikluk, 8

Military service. See Gurkhas

Money, place of, 46. See also Market economy

Mother-in-law, as source of marriage instability, 80, 107–8, 110, 114, 115, 119, 120, 122, 123–24, 125–26

Names, and forms of personal address, 121

Nationalism, of Limbu, 45–46, 48

Nepal, government of: attitude toward foreign researchers, 6–8; laws of, and Limbu marriage customs, 119; Limbu distrust of, 119. See also Limbuan

Newar, 2, 11, 16, 17, 18, 20, 40, 65

Nuclear family: in Limbuan, 50, 133; relationship of, to lineages and clans, 53–56. See also Clans; Extended family; Family; Household; Kinship; Lineage

Okwanama, 58

Pallo Kirat, 8

Panchthar, 8, 128

Patrilineal descent: and clans, 54–56; and inheritance of land, 49–53; and lineage, 53–54

Phalgunanda, and Limbu nationalism, 45–46

Phedap, 8, 128

Phidim, 17

Pignède, Bernard, 2

Pollution, ritual, 64; and lineage relationships, 53–54; of women during menstruation and after childbirth, 93, 98–99, 100

Polygyny, 67, 69, 126–27; and conflict between co-wives, 103–4, 109, 111–12, 114–16, 118, 126–27; as grounds for divorce, 126; and marriage instability, 118–19; Nepali law prohibiting, 119, 123

Pregnancy: beliefs about origins of, 93; rituals associated with, 93–96

Property. See Kipat; Land ownership; Raikar

Prythvi Narayan Shah, 34–35

Rai, 2, 8, 10, 16, 39; intermarriage with Limbu, 65; marriage patterns of, 128–29

Raikar, 35–36, 55

Religion: and festivals, 20–22; Limbu, compared to Hindu and Buddhist, 20, 43; and shamans, 22–24; and skepticism, 19; as way of life, 19–20

Research, anthropological: attitudes of Nepali government toward, 6–8; and case-history method, 5–6; and culture shock, 12–13; financing of, 6; political use of, by government agencies, 7; and problems in field, 30–32; suspicion of, by third-world nations, 7

Rice dance, 129; and marriage instability, 76–77; origins of, 73; role of, in courtship, 74–77, 78–79; and romantic love, 79; rules of, 73–77; and wedding ceremony, 77–78, 84, 91

Rice-eating ceremony, 98, 99–100

Rituals: of childbirth, 96–98; of death, 99; of pregnancy, 93–96; status of men in, 99–100, 131–32; status of women in, 93, 100, 131–32

Rosser, Colin, 2

Sagant, Philippe, 1, 6, 12, 39

Saimundri, 64, 67

Satya Hangma, and Limbu nationalism, 45–46

Satya Narayan, 58

Separation of spouses, and marriage instability, 112–13, 116, 118

Shamans, 56–58; diagnosis and cure of disease by, 23–24, 140; ritual roles of, 23, 43, 91–92, 94–96, 99

Sherpa, 2, 10–11

Songs, courtship, 79

Sorcerers, compared to shamans, 23–24

South Asia, marriage patterns and sexual roles in, 33–34, 132–34
Stomach ceremony, 93–96
*Sukha* (happiness), 13
Sunwar, 10–11

Tailors: role in wedding ceremony, 85, 92
Tagera Ningwaphuma, 20
Tamang, 10, 16, 18, 39
Tambar Khola, 8
Taplejung, 11, 12, 17
Tehrahum, 11, 12, 17; language in, 42
Tihar, 21–22, 43, 56, 73
Time: sense of, in Nepal, 13–14
Transportation: methods of, in Nepal, 7, 12
Trial marriage: Limbu marriage as form of, 5

Untouchable caste, 11, 20, 40, 41
Upadhiya Brahman, 39

Warokma Sammang, 94
Wedding ceremony, 72, 82–93; attire of bride and groom at, 85, 90; cost of, 80, 82–83; and drum dance, 84, 91; gifts at, 90; and rice dance, 77–78, 84, 91; season for, 80

Weekly markets, 17–19; and courtship customs, 73–79
Widows, 52; authority of, 70; land inheritance by, 69–70; remarriage of, 44, 67, 102–3, 109
Witches, compared to shamans, 23–24
Women in Limbuan: and adultery, 104–5, 110–11, 114–15, 122–23; age at first marriage, 80; central role in marriage stability, 128–29, 132; compared to South Asian women, 33–34, 132–34; daily routine of, 134–36; during pregnancy and childbirth, 93–98, 131–32, 136; as focus of anthropological study, 3–4; income generated by work of, 38–39; increased power within family of, 47–50, 70–71; and inheritance of land, 52–53, 69–70; languages used by, 42; in rituals, 56–58, 93, 100, 131–32; role of, in divorce, 120–29; and sickness and death of children, 136, 140; status and role of, 141–42; traditional subordination of, 69; work assigned to, 25–31, 141–42
Women in United States, 131–32

Yakha, 8
Yangarup, 8
Yashok, 17
Yuma Sammang, 20, 21, 56, 140